on Feet of Light

Pat Caffrey

The Angelic Council & Healers of LIGHT

Published in the United States of America by
LIGHT
46 Dog Hill Road
Dayville, CT 06241

First U.S. edition 2011

www.patcaffrrey.com

Book Design by Marie A. Carija
MACintegraldesign.com

ISBN 978-0-9840249-0-2

*I dedicate this book to three amazing souls —
my children — Brenda, Cari, & Tony. You reflect to me
the beauty of life. Thank you for showing me that life
goes on, change is a constant, and everything is possible.*

About the Author

Pat Caffrey is a representation of the Angelic Council & Healers of LIGHT. She dedicates her life to bringing their love, light and wisdom to you. She embodies this consciousness as she speaks their words and touches your soul. Her work is presented with group and private healing sessions and forums, worldwide. She is presently compiling this wisdom for publication.

See her @ www.patcaffrey.com

Prologue

I felt stuck in my life and although I knew it was time to move on, I had not been able to do so. I didn't know where to start. My marriage was all but over. I wanted to start a new career. I began to question everything. What did I really want? How could I accomplish it? Who was this new me that no longer fit into her old life?

Many things had occurred in the years leading up to this journey. Becoming disabled from my nursing career because of injuries to my back, resulting in paralysis, had left me deeply depressed. I had experienced four surgeries for this and when faced with the possibility of a fifth, I made another choice, took another path. A holistic approach and energy medicine entered the scene and my physical condition changed radically. My body healed, scar tissue thinned, and I found a flexibility I had never experienced before, both mentally and physically. I was given a new lease on life.

Vision improved. I discovered that as my "inner" vision improved, my physical vision followed suit. Becoming enthralled with the changes in my physical body, my scientific/analytical self wanted to know how these changes were happening. I studied Energy and Healing, Physics, Body-Oriented Psychology, Spirituality, and World Religions. I began to see how we create disease or we create healing in ourselves in each moment, by the choices we make.

I discovered that we are composed of energy and it must continue to flow to maintain health. I saw that our minds play a huge role in moving this energy. Energy follows thought. I found that we are also Spirit. We are connected to a greater whole that makes up the Universe we live in. I began to see

God as All That Is, not just an old man we see depicted with white hair, and I saw Him/Her in each of us. We are body, mind and spirit, all connected, all one. We are the trees, the sky; we are the Universe itself.

I needed to put this all together, to integrate this and see how these changes fit into my life. How did this affect me? Why had I experienced such seemingly miraculous events in my life? Why was I given this second chance to live my life as what I considered a viable, healthy woman? What was I to do with this? How could I give this back to others? I was searching, looking for answers.

I had become accustomed to meditating and connecting with a spiritual realm and identified with an "inner voice" that had become my guide. Although I identified this voice as my higher self, or God, I called this inner voice, this inner knowing, "The Guys." I found this to be a wonderful way of communicating with this consciousness, giving it character and personal identification. It is like having your best friends with you wherever you go.

I was getting used to having conversations with The Guys, and was learning to trust this guidance to be true for me. They guided this journey, and you will find our conversations and directions interspersed in the dialog as it progresses. These will be found in italics. There were times I trusted and times I did not. As you will see, the outcome of each choice was breathtakingly different.

I now look at this in retrospect and know this voice to be the voice of the Angelic Council and Healers of LIGHT. They sometimes speak as individuals and often are the combined energy of the whole. At the time of this trip however, I was being introduced to them and it was the beginning of a "friendship" that has changed my life completely. We have become inseparable. We are one.

One day, early that spring I began to hear that little voice inside saying I needed to take a trip to the Southwest, and I was told to study the terrain. I chose to start my journey in Albuquerque. This began a quest – Maps were studied, terrain was analyzed, and a general feel for the area began to take shape. Books of the area helped to put together a composite of that part of the country in a more complete picture. It now had color, shape, and form. I wasn't sure exactly why, but I trusted my inner guidance. Even though I questioned it in my head, it felt right in my heart and I knew I had to go.

One morning in June, I woke up knowing the time had come to make this a reality. The date of the actual trip was decided upon and a plane ticket purchased. As I was to find out during this adventure, when something is the exact right thing for you to do it will happen, so easily and quickly you will wonder how it occurred. The experience at the travel agency was one of those things. A ticket was found for approximately one quarter the usual fare. The agent had never seen this before and was reluctant to print the ticket; she didn't believe it would work. I had to convince her to do so. A similar thing happened for the rental car and everything I needed to purchase for the trip. I was to learn that these things happen often; they are like the signposts along our way that tell us we are in the right place, at the right time.

Preparations were made. Hiking equipment began to pile up, and clothes for the intense sun were gathered. I had decided to pack light and this meant taking only what I could carry on board the plane with me. That included carry on luggage with all my clothes, toiletries, and hiking gear. It took a while, but I finally succeeded in whittling down what I wanted to take, to the bare necessities.

The day of departure was set for July 17th and I was in a state of excitement. As the actual day approached, a feeling of anxiety began to creep in. Oddly enough, there was no actual fear that I was aware of. I knew this was a brand new experience for me, facing the unknown on a grand scale. I had never been away alone in a strange place before, yet I was oddly at peace with this process. I knew I would be facing many things I had never faced and would be learning much, not only about the places I would go and people I'd meet, but also about myself. I had no idea what an understatement that would turn out to be!

Day One
Taking flight

The day dawned cloudy and gray and there was a feeling of excitement in the air. Drops of rain began to fall on the wings as the plane left the ground, leaving the safety of my known world in its wake. As I watched out the rain-streaked window, I felt like a child in a candy shop. There were so many things in front of me, all of them new, and I wanted to taste every one of them. I also knew the step into the unknown would be a huge one. I was not sure what I was looking for or what I would find, but I knew it was time to find out. I also knew, without a shadow of a doubt, that my life would never be the same.

The first leg of the flight and layover were uneventful and smooth and I was deep in reverie when the plane began its descent. Outside the window, the wispy clouds sped past, the landscape becoming more and more pronounced as the plane slowly descended. Ridges of mountains ran north to south in two columns forming a trough between them. In this trough was a desert valley displaying signs of man. A city spread in the flat valley between the mountain ridges, a river running down its length outlined in green, painted on an otherwise brown canvas. I was approaching this city, on a journey to find myself.

I once heard it said that the pilgrim must take with him that which he seeks or he will not find it when he arrives. This would become clear to me in the weeks ahead. The journey is always the thing of importance. The destination is never quite attainable, always slightly out of reach.

The living canvas below slowly changed from an ethereal, nondescript landscape to a detailed place in my reality as we approached the earth. Watching the scene unfolding below as the plane approached the runway in this magical landscape, I was held captive to a story yet unwritten. I knew, in that place of knowing, that something extraordinary was about to happen in my life.

Touchdown brought on an experience of mixed emotions, excitement of playing out the part I had been planning, and the emotional mix of feelings coming to the forefront. I was beginning to feel the pangs of fear. Would I be able to do this? I was afraid of being alone. Feelings of insecurity were beginning to surface. I needed to face the fear.

Facing fears is the surest way I know to overcome them. It seldom seems easy, but the principle is simple. Face the fear, feel it in the deepest way possible in your body, and let it move through. The idea is that when we fully face the fear, it will no longer be there, or at least have lost its stranglehold on us. I believed this in principle and was about to find out how this worked in practice.

I was fortunate on this first day of my journey to find everyone I interacted with to be wonderfully helpful. Finding my way through the airport with all my present worldly possessions was a challenge. Getting on and off the airport bus with these belongings proved to be physically challenging and I was left with a rather large bruise on my shin, a reminder that it is OK to ask for help.

Once the rental car was secured, the heavy burden became a minor nuisance. Things were organized and separated into more manageable units. The collapsible cooler was set up and water purchased, to be my constant companion in this arid environment. The value of being organized was about to skyrocket to the priceless category.

The sky became ominous and lightning lit the sky. Huge areas of the heavens opened and poured down cool, cleansing drops of water, washing away the dust that covered the ground, a constant reminder of the climate. Was this a sign of what was to come? Would my old self be washed clean by the opening of the heavens within my being, shining light and bringing answers to my questions? I hoped this would be the case. It was the time of the "monsoons" in the desert, clear and sunny in the mornings, leading to clouds and rain in the evenings. It was a perfect time of contrasts and new beginnings.

The day was long and tiring, but I was energized in a unique way. The excitement of the journey was a constant reminder of where I was and what I had chosen to experience. Along with this was the fear that was quickly creeping into my awareness. I was no longer planning my journey, writing the script, I was entering into the experience of playing it out. Reality was setting in and I needed to sit, center myself, and examine the situation.

I found a motel and began to take stock of my situation. I was by myself in a place I had never been, and realized I was totally responsible for everything in my reality. There was silence, total and complete. As I sat alone on the bed and looked around, there was no other person to share the time, the space, or the moment. It was an initiation, coming face to face with myself in a totally different way, the first of many to come in the following days.

Had I been told what lay ahead, I would not have believed it. I did not have the reference for such an understanding. Such things are learned only by experience, they cannot be taught. So I sat there, fear filling my body with trepidation, wondering why I had come, wondering what lay ahead, both of these things unknown to me in the twilight of the moment. Had I made a mistake? Was I doing the right thing? The doubts were beginning to take hold in my mind.

I don't know how long I sat there feeling the emotions run through my being like a freight train, thoughts flashing by at light speeds, poking me and reminding me of my precarious place in the universe. We are huge in our total reality, body, mind and spirit, and yet we seem so insignificant in the actual experience. Humility met me in that room. It is easy to see what a tiny part we play when we sit in solitude of such magnitude.

As I sat in quiet and felt the connection to the greater realms, I began to feel the peace that comes from such awareness. It did not take away from the reality of my situation, but it gave me the courage to move forward, to face the unknown before me. We are body, mind, and spirit, all connected, all one. This awareness would help me through many days ahead as I learned more about how the totality of who we are fits into our every day experience, and how we create that reality. There were miles to go, things to do, and more to learn than I ever thought possible.

Conversation with The Guys:

Pat: Well, I'm here in Albuquerque. Now what do I do?

Guys: Take stock of where you are. Did you find anything today especially interesting?

Pat: Yes; I was mesmerized by the mountains when I flew into Albuquerque. I could see the flat desert all around, with the mountain ridges going north to south. The river ran down the middle of the mountains with a large span of desert between them. I've seen it on the maps and been curious about how it ran through the state and I saw it from the air. It was spectacular.

Guys: Know this well. Know that you only saw a very small portion of it. Remember what it looked like from the air as you go south to Alamagordo and White Sands. The view is similar.

Pat: In what direction shall I go first?

Guys: We will see when you get up in the morning. We do not want you thinking about what your next move will be. Tonight you rest and take stock of where you are. Breathe in the energy. Let go of everything. We know how difficult this day has been. Do not add to it at this time. Tomorrow will be soon enough. Do what helps you relax. FEEL what you are feeling and let it move through. There is energy that needs to be released before you go tomorrow.

Thoughts and fears of all magnitude were swirling around in my mind during that night. There was a fear of looking like a fool, going on this journey and finding nothing. I had always found "eating crow" particularly distasteful and there were a few people back home that thought this trip a less then brilliant endeavor. I knew I would be led on this journey, as I was led to prepare for it, and I was afraid of not hearing The Guys and missing the clues along the way. I knew a large part of this journey was about learning to trust myself, to know that part of me that connected to a higher place, to listen to that inner voice, to God. I was afraid of letting people down; there were a lot of people who believed I would make this journey a personal success story. This brought up a lot of self-worth issues. Could I do it? Would I succeed, without running home in what I perceived as defeat? Would I fail? Even though I knew that failure is only a judgment put on oneself, that all failure is self-judgment, I still felt the fear.........................
and so I faced the fear.

Lesson from the day: Face your fear

Fear is fear. No matter what name you put on it, it is still the same energy and can be approached in the same way. Mine for the day had many names – Unknown – Alone – Insecure – Failure – Self-worth, etc. You need to face the fear (a low vibration) and allow it to transform to a higher vibration of love and light. Following just a few simple steps can do this. This will also work with any other emotion.

1. The way I find best to deal with fear is to face it directly. To do that, you first need to be honest with yourself and admit your deepest feelings and own them as your own. This is not always as easy as you like, but crucial to the process. You have to let go of any sense of judgment for having the fear (or any other emotion). If you won't own the emotion you feel, there is no way to feel it fully and allow for the process to happen.

2. Find a quiet place and allow yourself to feel the feeling as deeply as possible. Allow yourself to feel it in every part of your body. Watch it. Notice what you notice. Do not judge it.

3. Do not allow yourself to get caught up in the story. Emotions are feelings built around a story. Without the story you attach to the emotion, there is just the energy of the feeling. Forget your childhood or any event in your life connected to the feeling. Just feel the feeling!

4. Allow the energy of the feeling to flow and move. When you do this you let it free from your body. It is stored in your DNA and this is the key to unlock it.

5. Notice as it changes to something else. The feeling

may lessen or move to another place or it may disappear completely. What matters it that it is no longer what it was. Allow it to flow until it changes to a feeling that is different and hopefully more peaceful.

6. Let it go. Forget it. Know that it is done. If you find your self reliving the story again, recognize it as old habit and let it go!

Day Two
A new way of seeing my world

The fears of last night seemed distant, although still there, lurking quietly in the background. This day started as the rest would, by sitting in silence and connecting with God, the Universe, All That Is. I sensed and heard that this day would be about *feelings*. I was to just head out in a direction that felt right and see where it brought me. I was to take this one step at a time. I was to use my feelings as my guide and trust them to bring me where I needed to be.

Intending to go north, to Santa Fe, you can imagine my surprise when I found myself headed west. I had no idea why, except that it *felt* right. As I did this I began to laugh to myself, even at myself. Here I was in a land in which I was unfamiliar, driving on roads I knew nothing of, because I had a feeling it was right. I was allowing God, The Guys, that little voice in my heart, to guide me. Who would believe this? I wasn't even sure I did.

The unnumbered boulevard stretched before me like a runway of sorts, wide and flat, cut into a brown desert landscape. In the distance it rose and dipped over rolling hills, slowly disappearing into the landscape. It was an awesome sight, a path leading into the unknown. How prophetic it seemed at the time. As I crossed the river silently meandering down the valley floor, the Rio Grande, the terrain ahead began to raise up like the back of an ancient creature, a dinosaur, long since extinct, returning to lead me home.

Reaching the top of that silent beast brought yet another surprise. The road stopped abruptly at a fence, an enclosure resembling a military installation. There were two choices, take the road to the right, an unmarked road, narrow and not highly traveled, or turn around and go back. The road to the right felt like the right choice, so I took it. Much to my surprise, this brought me to the interstate highway leading to Santa Fe.

I was to learn that there are no mistakes in this world, in this Universe. When we learn to trust in ourselves, we begin to see that there are reasons for everything that happens. It may not seem evident at the time, but it is nevertheless so. Taking a road in the desert seemed like a mechanical action, yet when looked at from a different perspective, it was a lesson worth a thousand words. Trusting my Self brought me to exactly the place I had planned to go. The destination was the same, the difference was the path and the lesson learned on the journey to get there.

How often had I gone through life without a thought of how or why things happened? How often did I take things for granted? I was beginning to experience the connection of all things. There are no mistakes. And I was learning to let go of the outcome. By letting go of the outcome, the destination, we open ourselves to all possibility, all the wondrous miracles in between. We must relearn to be a child and see through those eyes, the eyes of wonder, and feel the love of the moment, the anticipation and sheer joy of exploration.

Life is filled with such wonder. Do we see it? I had not, for I believed life kept me busy. I had forgotten that life does not happen to us, but through us. We create our own lives in each moment, by each choice we make. We need to stand back and look at what is there. Really look. Stand back and see it from another perspective. See how it fits into the whole of our lives, not just the present moment. The picture that begins to unfold before us is a masterpiece, created by our own genius, our own choices in each and every moment.

The masterpiece of my life, although I would not have called it such at that moment, was beginning to unfold before me. I saw a canvas, painted in a palette of colors that had become faded. What did it need? How do you change a canvas, painted with colors that were perfect for the time of the painting, but now outdated? What painting did I want to create now? These were all questions beginning to seep into my consciousness, my awareness of the now, the moment in which we experience all things.

Watching the terrain change as I drove became a fascination. Passing through the foothills, was another lesson in change. Nothing stays the same, even in a relatively small area, just as nothing in our lives stays the same from moment to moment. Change is the natural flow of life. Flat desert became large hills and deeper valleys, covered with denser, taller vegetation. The temperature dropped a few degrees and the air felt different in some way as I approached Santa Fe.

I decided to *feel* my way to the plaza, to trust that I would be guided and know the way, another test of this ability to find my way in a new place. Oddly enough, I found myself driving directly to the plaza, buildings built in a square around a beautiful park. This was done without aid of a map. Traffic was heavy and there were few parking areas available so I chose to trust there would be one where I needed it. As I approached the square, a car directly on the corner of the plaza pulled out of its space, leaving me an opening, a gift from the Universe.

I had imagined that I would spend a few days in Santa Fe. I shopped for some essentials and as I walked, felt the energy of the area. As I let the feelings of that energy vibrate in my body, I felt uncomfortable, hemmed in, and knew it was time to leave. I was tired, hot and had no idea where I was going, but I felt the need to go south. I headed in that direction using the trusty map, and got hopelessly lost.

The streets in the upper canyon were narrow and winding, snaking through the hills like some large, uncoiled serpent. Adobe buildings of wondrous earth colors, built on exposed beams, lined the streets. It was a magical place, perhaps reminiscent of old Mexico, or at least an older time in this place.

Suddenly, ahead of me in the middle of the street stood a man. He asked if I needed help and I told him I was lost. He went to a car, got out some paper and drew me a map. He then disappeared into a studio, one of the buildings along that street. He was gone as quickly as he appeared. If it had not been for the directions in my hand, I would have thought I imagined him. The directions were superb and I soon found myself back on the main road.

I asked The Guys what had just happened and was given this answer: "Even when you feel lost and alone, there is always someone there to help you find your way." I realized this man was just the visible example, put here for me to see. We are never alone, although we may feel this way when we are being private, apart from other people. When we "go inside", when we allow ourselves to feel connected to the greater source, call it God, Allah, Yaweh, Wakan Tanka, Brahman, The Universe, The Great I AM, or whatever name we know Him/Her/It by; we will never be alone, can never be alone.

Up until then I had not allowed myself to feel the fear that was lying dormant below the surface. It was mid afternoon and I felt a need to head south, which would bring me to Roswell. This meant a trip of about 200 miles or so, through barren desert with almost no civilization. Fear bubbled to the surface. What if the car broke down? What if I ran out of gas? There were a thousand things running through my head.

The mind can be a terrible thing. It can take a thought and before we know it, have us frozen in fear. I chose to use my mind to create new possibilities, to allow my heart to lead my mind, instead of the other way around. Without doing that, this adventure would not have been possible. This day was about trusting my feelings, which come from the heart, and I was not about to lose that to my mind and my fear.

That decision made, I headed into the desert thinking there were no more wonderful things that would happen that day. I was mistaken. The road out of the foothills was as impressive as the road into them. The steep green and brown hills and valleys slowly became rolling brown hills with shorter vegetation and I drove, mesmerized by the view. As I came over a hill I pulled over and stopped, stunned by the sight. In front of me, as far as the eye could see, stretched the desert, so awesome in its scope it took my breath away.

Road to Roswell

This canvas was painted in shades of browns and reds, earth tones with splotches of green. The sky stretched beyond imagination, unimpeded by the man-made world. In the distance were huge areas of dark clouds with streaks of lightning shooting from their cores like fire shooting from the nostrils of long forgotten dragons. A magical world of wonder spread before me and I followed it like the Yellow Brick Road to Oz. Checking once again with the feelings within my being, I found the fear was gone. Instead, in its place was a feeling of peace, love, and, for lack of a better term, home. It felt like *home*.

Being monsoon season, the sides of the road were prolific with wildflowers, something I had not expected to find in the desert. There were flowers of yellow and green galore, all raising their heads to the sky, joyful in their short-lived experience of life in this harsh environment. I felt the joy, the elation of that life and of my own, and the privilege of sharing their moment in time and space. The rain also had an effect on the temperature. I had prayed before I started the journey that I would be able to stand the heat of the desert; monsoon season answered my prayer.

The car was the only glitch of that day, it developed a problem with the front wheel and was pulling to the left, quite badly by the time I reached Roswell. I knew the car would need to be dealt with before going any further. Pulling into town that evening was both a relief and sadness that the day was over. It had been a magical day of discovery.

I was beginning to understand that there is a consciousness in the Universe that is a part of us and all we have to do is tap into it, to trust this within ourselves. All the answers are within us. All the wisdom of the Universe is ours for the asking and it takes only the act of listening, feeling what it feels like in our hearts and bodies, and then trusting what we feel.

In hopes of hiking in the desert, I asked the girl at the motel desk if she knew a place to hike. So far, every bit of desert I had seen was fenced in. She told me her mother had hurt her back and her "spiritual doctor" told her to hike in the desert by herself. The place she hiked was near town and she told me how to get there. It just kept amazing me that, whatever I needed to know, the answer was there for me in the most obvious of ways. There are no mistakes, nothing happens by chance, and all things are connected.

Although the day had been tiring and the day seemed long, the experience was breathtaking. The vista was superb and the people perfectly placed to see what I needed to see. Choosing to trust in my heart instead of my head/mind and my rigid beliefs, I had opened myself to experience things I would have never thought possible. Every time I needed to know something, the exact right person was put in my path. Each time I doubted and fell into old habits, I became lost. The lessons were many and magnificent. I was learning to feel the truth in my heart and was beginning to feel an intimacy with my inner guidance.

Conversation with The Guys:

Pat: What a day. Whoever said the shortest distance between two points is a straight line was correct, however; this is not turning out to be my experience. Today I went in a loop.

Guys: We gave you little to go on when we told you today was "test day". We led you first west out of Albuquerque, which you did not expect, and, then to Santa Fe as you had hoped. These were tests of your trust and you heard and followed us well. We then asked how you liked the energy of your desired destination.

Pat: It was strange. It is my favorite spot, but I couldn't wait to leave. It felt stifling and chaotic. I sensed I was to go south and then drove about 200 miles in the most spectacular scenery I have yet to see. There was bright blue sky and cotton ball clouds to my back and both sides, and I drove continu-

ally toward dark, lightning streaked skies. It was awesome. It is strange to see a green desert with wildflowers coming up along the road. They only last a short time when the rains come, so I feel blessed to have been here at this time.

Guys: You have been wondering why you are here. It is now time to tell you. You have come here to learn about yourself and to let go of the remaining fear in your body. We are with you as we always are. Nothing has changed but the location. Fear not that you will miss us and you will go home "empty handed". This will not happen.

You are entering a phase in your life where things are becoming clearer and clearer. We know it does not feel that way at this time, but it will soon. There were some things that needed to be cleared from your body memory. It is reaching a point of clearance at this time. Let the energy move through. All is well.

Lesson from the day: Trust your Feelings

Trust is something most people have a difficult time with. You believe that it entails giving something up, usually your own beliefs. This is not true at all. Trust is not a separation, but an inclusion of all things. It is a knowing in the deepest part of your being that all is perfect. How do you trust? You already do. You either trust that what you have learned is true or you choose to trust in a higher consciousness that you can tap into. You trust things will work for the best or you choose to trust they will work for the worst. At all times, you trust in one or the other.

If I had chosen to trust in my past conditioning, I would have continued using the map, been fearful of becoming lost, and not seen the wonderful things around me. I would have spent all my time being concerned about time and what ifs. I would have been so caught up in trusting nothing but myself, I would have missed the experience of a lifetime. By trusting a power greater than myself, by choosing to trust in the feelings in my heart, I knew I was safe. I was then free to enjoy all that was around me, seeing with eyes that were completely open and not jaded with old ideas and beliefs.

Old beliefs are good for the person who taught them to us. They are only part of our present experience if we choose them to be. Some are limiting beyond belief and only when we choose to put our trust in what we feel in our hearts will we be able to discover who and what we truly are. To experience the truth of who we are, is to experience love and life itself.

Next time you're in a situation that requires trusting your feelings and making a choice, consider these few important rules:

1. Look honestly at the choices before you. See the situation as it truly is, not as you want it to be.

2. Are you trusting old beliefs and dogma that has been taught to you or are you trusting to make your choice because it feels good in your own heart?

3. Don't be afraid to disappoint another to be true to yourself.

4. Make sure the choice you put your trust in represents the highest version of who you are and your heart's desire. If it "feels right," trust in that.

5. Make no mistake – you will choose to trust in something and your choice will determine the experience you have.

Please choose to trust what represents the highest version of who you are at the moment. It will determine not only your experience, but also what comes back to you from that experience.

Day Three
One with the Universe

What a difference a day makes. Went to bed on day two in a state of well-being and contentment. Woke up on day three with terror filling my very being. I felt a bone crushing loneliness and my body felt like it would die. The fear I had been burying beneath the surface came rushing out in a torrent.

Sitting in silence and contemplating the feelings within, the fear began to calm to a workable level. I was no longer frozen in the fear, but ready to use it to propel myself forward. It is not the absence of fear that makes us able to survive and thrive, but the use of it when it becomes overpowering. Facing the fear lessens it, makes it manageable, and before we know it, it is gone, no longer a threat. Running from the fear and burying it will only keep it active, ready to resurface and strike when we least expect it. It was again time to face it and deal with it.

The day had dawned cloudy and not too hot, perfect for hiking. I donned my hiking gear and prepared to embark on my journey. Although I knew I needed to do this, I was afraid of going out there by myself. Visions of creepy, crawly things ran in my mind, threatening to take hold of my actions. This inner battle raged until the heart finally rose above the mind.

Finding the place I was told about, I parked the car, took a deep breath, faced the fear, and walked into the desert. A few sayings come to mind – face the fear, fake it till you make it, and just do it! All were appropriate. It's been said that the first step is the biggest, the hardest of all. I believe this to be true, for this is the step that takes us into the unknown. This was my first step for day three, and it was HUGE.

I stood in a somewhat hilly area in the desert, on a high perch at the edge of a cliff overlooking a shallow pond. Deep crevices, rich in red rock and soil scarred the surface. Standing above them, it was possible in places to look between my feet and see through the cracks in the surface to the deep valley below. The sky stretched to the ends of the horizon. Clouds of ever changing shape drifted overhead, leaving scattered shadows on the ground.

Bottomless Lakes State Park, Roswell

Not knowing my purpose, other than feeling a deep need to be there, I stood looking at the sky, praying and asking why I had been sent to this particular spot on that particular day. Gazing at the sky, connecting with that inner place, I began to hear the familiar voice, feel the inner knowing. I was told to take off whatever I was wearing that I felt comfortable without. I shed my gloves, long sleeved over shirt, hat, backpack, dark glasses, and walking stick. Left only in pants, tank top and hiking boots, I stood alone in this desert, face to the heavens and hands to the sky, in supplication to God. I would have felt foolish, but it felt right in my heart, so I stood, and waited, and listened to the stillness.

I found myself repeating, out loud, a promise I made to God several years before. I promised to be His hands, His eyes, His mouth, and His ears. I promised to be whatever He needed me to be in this time and place in the Universe. And then I wept – alone in the desert, before God and the Universe. It was a cleansing stream of tears, a catharsis, taking away all the fear and doubt of that morning, washing away mountains of debris, collected and stuffed for what seemed like eons.

I prayed for strength and courage, for help in knowing my path. What was I to do? Where was I to go? I prayed out loud and heard the words spoken in my voice and foreign tongue, uniquely reminiscent of Native American. Somehow this did not seem strange, but oddly familiar. Something in my peripheral vision caught my attention and a deer bounded by my side as if in slow motion, watching me as I watched her. I felt connected to this wonder of creation, as if words were spoken; I was accepted in her world. Three birds of prey circled overhead around me in smaller and smaller, and then larger and larger circles, finally soaring off to the distant heavens, one by one, and disappearing from view.

I stood in wonder, in awe of this experience. I had no explanation of the event, yet it felt totally natural, as if this sort of thing happened every day. I shared the gratefulness for this experience with All That Is and I sat on the ground, breathing in the air and what felt like the Universe itself. I felt blessed, loved, and connected to the scene before me, not like I was watching it, but that I was a part of it. There was no separation between it and myself. We were all energy, swaying to a dance of creation, all connected, all one.

I sat there for some time before I could once again stand

and leave this place. As I walked, large swarms of grasshoppers of all shapes and description flew up around me. Swarms of yellow, green and brown rose up and buzzed about me, encasing me in clouds of life. I had never before had such an experience, and have not again since. Such sharing, such living examples of joy come few times in a person's life. It is necessary, paramount, that we take hold of each one. Recognize each one for the miracle it is and take it in, make it a part of who we are. Live the miracle. Be the miracle.

As it had been challenging to go into the desert, it was more challenging to leave it. Such an experience is not left easily. I wanted to stay there, to hold onto it. I discovered that you can never leave such wonder; you take it with you. It is never gone. It will live with me forever, for it became a part of me. Remembering an experience makes it happen again; we re-live it in the moment of memory. It is no longer a thing of the past, but yet a present experience, lived once again in the now.

Now is all there is. What happened in the past, when it happened, happened in the now, the present moment of experience. What will happen in the future will happen in the now when it occurs. There is never a time we experience that is not in the present. Life is one eternal string of now moments, one connecting to the next in perfect harmony and balance.

Getting back to the more mundane things, it was time to see about the car. Luckily, there was an office for the rental agency in town, so I brought the car to them. They were not able to fix it, so they gave me a different one. I laughed when I was given the "Escort", as it would be my escort for more miles than I would imagine.

The afternoon proved to be more interesting than anticipated. I had imagined the International UFO Museum and Research Center in Roswell to be somewhat of a tourist trap, sensationalized with all sorts of things to monopolize that interest. I was pleasantly surprised. It was seriously done and contained much information I had not been aware of about the 1947 "Roswell Incident," a supposed UFO crash in the area. There were displays of newspaper articles printed at the time of the incident, showing both sides of the controversy, as well as reports of a survivor that lived for several days and eyewitness accounts to many details. There was also an area dedicated to crop circles, which I found to be quite fascinating, and best of all was the Showtime movie "Roswel," done by several well-known actors who depicted the scene in a very realistic manner. Overall, it was very impressive.

The events of the afternoon left me with more questions. Did this crash really happen? Are we alone in the Universe? There has been much controversy over this subject. Some believe there is intelligent life out there, some do not. I had always believed there is, and this just added to that belief. It is inconceivable to me that we are all there is. Could God have made this astronomical universe and then only put life on this one tiny planet? I don't think so. Can we be the most intelligent species in the Universe, the most loving? I refuse to believe that.

When you feel a connection to the whole, feel a part of All That Is, it changes the way you see things. You are no longer separate from the rest of the Universe, AND you feel the life in all other parts. What you are connected to is not blank, empty. What is it? What's out there? I have a feeling one-day we will know, but that is my own belief, my own perception based on my own feelings and experience. Everyone will be his or her own judge of this, in his or her own way, adopted from personal experience. As for myself, I knew I would never look at the sky the same way again.

That evening was spent in reflection. So many things had

happened in such a short time that I needed to allow it all to sink in, to find that space of comfort within myself. There was a pool at the motel and I went there and watched the children. There is something magical about watching the freedom and abandon of their actions. They do not question everything they do; they just do it with joy. That evening they swam, they splashed and they laughed as if the world were uproariously funny. I had to agree.

The world is not always the serious place we see; it is our reactions to it that make it so. There is no built in meaning to anything that happens. If ten people watch an event, there will be ten different reactions and interpretations of that event. All things happen through us, for us to see our own reactions. The world is our mirror. We too often, when we don't like what we see in the mirror, try to change the mirror instead of ourselves. If the mirror frowns, it is not the fault of the mirror. We must first smile into it, so it is a smile we will see returned.

These children taught me a lot in those precious moments. We need to take things less seriously at times, to forget the worries and burdens we have placed on ourselves and let go. We need to enjoy the simple things and feel the pure joy of excitement, just as those children did as I watched. They live in the moment, without worry or care about tomorrow or the next day. Can we do that? I had not been able to. I had much to learn.

Retiring for the night, I thought about my route for the next day. I wanted to go to Alamagordo and thought about a southern route through the mountains. It looked like the most interesting way to go and I thought it would be relaxing. When I meditated on this, put this in my heart, I kept hearing the word "Ruidoso," over and over, like a song stuck on repeat. That would mean taking a different route. You know what it's like when you get a song playing over and over in your mind, and you can't get it out? I thought that's what was happening. It played over and over in my mind, but I ignored it; I didn't want to go that way. I decided to sleep on it and see what happened in the morning.

Conversation with The Guys:

Pat: I feel like I'm in a whirlwind of emotions and don't know what to do with them. My fears have been popping up all over the place. I don't understand what is happening and I feel very confused.

Guys: The experience you had in the desert this morning is just a prelude to what is to come. Fear not. This trip is not for nothing. We tell you now to have faith: trust in the plan, the process and yourself. Allow the fear that is left in the body to move through. Do not stuff it down when it pops up, but let it move freely. At this moment we recommend that you find ways to enjoy yourself. Do whatever feels good to you in the moment.

Be kind to yourself. Rest. Relax.

You wondered what the language was that you spoke this morning in the desert — it is an ancient tongue that would be called "early" Native American. It was understood. Your spirit knows this. It is perfect.

You will know more soon my dear one, soon indeed.

Open yourself to all possibility. Let go of all preconceptions and fears of what you think this should be. We know you came with some expectations, even as we told you not to. It is OK, but paramount that you release them now. Be open. Be empty. Allow All That Is to be, as was the case in the desert this morning. The deer and birds brought you love and acceptance my dear one. More than you imagine at this time. You are one.

Lesson from the Day:
Connecting with All That Is

We all feel alone in our world at times. Because we are physical beings, we see ourselves as separate from everyone and everything around us. Although this is not true, we are here to experience it as such. We chose to be human and experience being separate so we can see that we are not. Contradiction? Yes – and no.

We chose to become human and inhabit a physical body. We came here with the purpose of re-membering who we truly are. We are a spiritual being, a soul, having a physical experience in this universe. Most of you reading this book already know this, but what does that mean to you? Are you consciously living this or are you living your lives from a perspective that your physical body is who you are? Think about this before you give yourself an answer.

Every time we have a pain, we fear the power the body has over us. Every illness brings fear of what will happen to us. We give more power to the body with some diseases than others. Cancer. Heart disease. These are things we believe have control over our world. What if you turned that around and connected to your true essence? How do you think this would change your life? Let's try an experiment to see what would happen if you did exactly that.

1. Find a quiet place by yourself. Perhaps some soft music playing in the background. Maybe for you it's a peaceful place in the forest or sitting by the ocean. Choose what is best for you.

2. Notice what is happening in your body. Feel any place that draws your attention. Don't judge what you notice. If it's pain or discomfort, allow it to be there. Just be an observer of it.

3. Listen to the sounds around you. Feel the sweetness and
    peace of your surroundings. Allow that feeling to become
    your whole focus. Hear the music, the birds, the stream,
    the ocean or whatever you have chosen to be around you.
    Use your mind to think of the most loving moment
    in your life and let that expand.

4. Feel the peace in your heart. Feel the connection to some
    thing else that is not explainable in your world. Know
    you are not alone.

5. Notice what happens to the feeling in your body that
    first drew your attention. Is it there when you connect
    to the energy that is the true you? It is not, because you
    are well and healthy in your true state. There is no
    illness, no pain and no sorrow. There just IS the being-
    ness of your soul.

Practice this in every situation, whenever you can. Bring
this to work with you. In-corporate this into your physical
experience. You are not this or that. You are this AND that.

Day Four
Feeling the Energy

Morning came with a promise of joyful expectation. Perhaps it was the light coming in the window, or perhaps it was all the things worked through in the dream state, but something had changed. The fears of yesterday were not present in that moment. Listening to the silence within brought me the route for the day. The word Ruidoso was now shouted in my ear, there would be no doubt about my path for that day. I did not know why, but I trusted there was a reason to take that route.

There had been times in my life when I heard that little voice guiding me and I had not listened. Each time this happened, I found myself wishing I had. It is not that we don't have this innate guidance; it is that we don't listen, or if we do, we discard it as not being important, or a figment of our imagination. Yesterday's lesson was bright in my mind and I chose to trust this inner knowing.

It seemed that today would also be about feelings, but with an added twist. Not only would I be asked to feel what choices seemed right, but to feel the actual energy around me. When we interact with someone or some place, we are actually able to feel the person or place. When we close our eyes and feel what's in our bodies, we can feel it in many ways. It may be a feeling of comfort or discomfort, ease or unease, or a desire to stay or leave. As we practice this it becomes easier to understand what we are feeling.

The road stretched ahead for miles. Open, brown desert, speckled with sage and other low growing green plants lay on a flat section of earth. The hills in the distance stood like rims of a bowl, containing all I could see, including myself. Soft music drifted from the tape deck, creating a slightly ethereal quality to the scene. Being alone in that moment was not a challenge, but a blessing. Peace settled over me like a warm blanket as the scene sped by like frames of a film passing by the window. I was part of an interactive canvas, pliant and moveable, swaying once more to the dance of life.

Ruidoso is a beautiful town in the mountains, its claim to fame being its racetrack, casinos, and Fox Caves, Billy the Kid's hideout. The mountains are covered with huge pine trees, giving the impression I was back in the northeast where I grew up. From a larger perspective of Earth, it's as if a giant hand reached down into the desert, grabbed a handful of Earth and raised it to the sky. This section took on a life of its own and grew different vegetation. Its climate became cooler, its animals different, and its people adapted to a different environment. And all of this exists within the confines of the desert. Our world is truly amazing! When we think it is not, we need to look from a different angle, a different perspective. We need to step back from the canvas, just as the great painters have done for millennia, so the paint strokes disappear from our vision and the total picture takes shape, the details disappearing.

Going through Ruidoso was uneventful and I began to question why I had listened to my inner voice. Was it my imagination? Had I made a mistake? Did I interpret it correctly? As I drove down the western side of the mountains, through the Mescalero Apache Reservation, I began to feel a very comfortable feeling, like I knew this place, or had been there before. I had no idea why, so I just acknowledged the feeling and allowed myself to feel it as deeply as I could. Acknowledging unknown feelings is the first step to discovering who we are.

As I drove down the mountain, I saw a small building standing by itself in the edge of the woods. It was a shop of some sort and had a sign written in the native language. The Guys asked me what I "felt" as I passed this building and I felt a sadness, but it was filled with pride. It felt **proud**. I was getting the message that I had to turn around and go back to this shop and tell the person inside what I just experienced. I heard my inner voice affirming this action, it felt like the right thing to do, and yet I almost didn't do it. My mind kicked in with all kinds of things like "What, are you crazy?" They're going to think I'm nuts!

I thought of many things that would keep me from going back. Then I thought, "Oh well, no one there knows me. So what if I make a total fool of myself?" I turned around and went back. The shop was filled with wonderful things of interest, such as beading supplies and Native American Apache crafts. The woman who ran the shop was there by herself. I didn't know how to start this conversation, so I just came out with it. I told her what occurred when I drove by and that I needed to tell her the word proud, or pride. I figured she would think I was crazy, but continued the story.

She looked at me with a puzzled look and said that Apaches are a proud race, so maybe that is why this happened. OK, I could buy that. At least she didn't kick me out or call for the "little men in white coats." Then she looked at me, really looked, as if deciding how much to say. Tears welled up in her eyes, her voice softened, and she told me a story. The name of her shop had been *Apache Pride* and two close family members had died not long ago, prompting her to change the name. She continued to tell me the story of her family and I felt a connection to her that was very unique.

We looked into each other's eyes and saw something there that went beyond strangers. There was recognition of something more, deeper, closer. The air around me felt charged with an energy I never noticed before. We had shared something special. Looking into another's eyes connects us, makes us a part of each other. To avoid contact is to separate ourselves, allowing us to fool ourselves into thinking we are better than or less than they are.

It was a moment I would not have missed for the world, although I almost did because of my own judgment of myself, and fear of how I would look to others. How many times do we feel like we would like to speak to someone we meet? How many times do we actually follow through on it? It is not something I had done often. I also knew in that moment that I would no longer choose fear as my guide. Not only did I have a message for her; she had one for me. She taught me to trust my instincts and to have the courage to follow through on them.

We are all living our own private lives and they are being played out with others. Nothing is by chance. We need to take the time, make the time to communicate with others in our lives. See not only what part they play, but what part we play for them. Life is a perfect orchestration, a perfect dance, and yet we pass it by. This woman reflected to me, who I am, and showed me that we are all connected. As I was able to trust, so she opened her own trust to me. What we give out we get back.

Had I not listened to The Guys shouting "Ruidoso", I would not have taken that route, and if I had driven by, I would have missed that wondrous opportunity to learn from this gifted teacher. As we live our every day lives, we learn and we teach. We are both teacher and student in each moment of every day. Because of her I will remember that lesson. I have a whistle she made sitting on display in my home, a constant reminder to trust in myself, and to remember that we are not alone. There is another force in this Universe that connects us to each other. We need only remember how to feel it, hear it, and use it in our lives.

I was overwhelmed and grateful beyond belief for this lesson. As a matter of fact, the meeting was so huge for me, I thought it would be my only lesson for the day. Again, my penchant for understatement was to be proved. There was more to come.

As I drove into the foothills I was stunned to feel the energy in that area. I felt sadness and grief so overwhelming in its intensity I could barely drive. Pulling over, I allowed the feeling to move through and I heard a voice that seemed to come from the Earth itself say "They tried to kill us". This time I also saw a picture in my mind, a huge mushroom cloud. I realized that the valley now spread before me contained the Trinity Site, the place the atomic bomb had been tested.

Not knowing what to do with this, I sat in silence and connected with that place inside that holds all the answers, the wisdom of the Universe. In my mind I saw a column of light coming from the sky, shining bright white light on the earth. I expanded it to shine on the entire area surrounding me, which included the mountains, foothills, and valley. Slowly, the feeling of sadness and grief lessened and I could once again continue.

What had just happened? Is it possible to feel the energy of a place? Yes. All things are made up of energy and all of them have a vibration that is unique to them. This goes for people as well as land and objects. Each of us has our own unique frequency or vibration, called our signature vibration. It is like an energetic fingerprint and is one way we recognize each other. We are more than just physical beings. Land holds a vibration also, as I was to learn in the days ahead.

I was looking over the southern end of the Tularosa Valley, viewed from the higher elevation, and it brought its own rewards. The valley stretched below, north to south, filled with pure white gypsum. Sunlight sparkled on it like diamonds on a bed of glass. Had I not known the terrain and history of the valley, I would have thought it to be water. It was possible to imagine an ancient traveler, heading for the much-needed water in the desert, never to get there. I learned to appreciate the illusion of a mirage at that moment.

What we see is not always what we think it is. It is easy to look at something and believe we are correct. It registers in our minds that what we see is real. Is it? Had I not known, I would have believed this was water. What other things in my life had I seen that were not what I thought? How many disagreements had I taken part in where I fought for my belief of what was real? Was my view of what was real, real for others? Looking at life from this perspective shifted my beliefs of reality. What is it? Once again I found myself with more questions than answers. This was turning out to be quite an adventure indeed, and in deed.

My mind was swirling with thoughts when I arrived in Alamagordo, a large town that stretches along the edge of the valley floor. The rains had held off for a few days and it was very hot, the sun reflecting off the white gypsum dunes. I was hot, tired and in need of a break. I took advantage of the afternoon and wrote postcards, walked, and enjoyed the scenery. It was a respite from the driving, and I treated myself to a much needed, leisurely meal. There are times we need to put aside our busy schedules and take a break. By evening I felt renewed in body and spirit.

There is a place near Alamagordo, called White Sands National Monument. It contains two hundred and seventy five square miles of gypsum dunes, the ones seen from the mountainside earlier in the day. A ranger would be guiding a tour at dusk and a talk on the stars would be taking place after dark. I decided to go.

You might think there are only so many things of wonder a person can take in, in one day. I found there is no limit. We are capable of unimaginable feats and creations and our ability to accumulate information and experience is boundless.

Driving into the dunes is what you might imagine in a science fiction movie. The dunes are pure white, high as houses, and in constant motion. The roads are plowed to keep them passable in the ever-shifting white sand. Children arrive with saucer sleds, to slide down the sides of the steep slopes, as if on mountains of snow. It is a magical place, a landscape void of buildings and any signs of man, other than a few amenities and the roads for access.

Once again I found my definitions being challenged. A desert had a certain picture in my mind and it was not this: and yet this was desert. Definitions are very limiting and keep us from growing if we are not willing to see beyond them. When we label something we stop it from being something else and so we miss what is there. I realized I needed to expand my way of thinking, my way of looking at things and categorizing them. All things are unique; there are no two alike. Just because one desert has brown or red dirt, that does not mean they all do.

There is a fascinating property of gypsum. It does not get hot like regular sand. The ranger surprised the group she was leading by telling us we could hike it in our bare feet. This was another challenge to my mind. It did not fit the picture I had of hiking in the desert. I put that aside and took the challenge. It was marvelous, a cool, powdery sand that forms around the feet in perfect comfort. I felt like a child in a giant sandbox.

It is an extremely harsh environment, as the strong winds move the dunes in an ever-changing landscape. The plants and animals of the desert fought to live in this environment and many did not survive. A few have evolved and adapted but not many. I fell in love with this place. Its beauty was staggering and there was a quality about it that defied imagination. I knew I would never again be able to live within the definitions or boundaries I placed on things. I could no longer create boxes to put things in, each neatly in its place in my orderly mind.

The sun set in the west behind the San Andres Mountains with a beautiful display, fire shining through dark streaking clouds, in a never ending sky. Viewing this from the top a dune was a humbling experience. I felt so small in the total scheme of things. It was like sitting on top of the world, watching creation itself. It was breathtaking and I felt stunned. I felt the energy around me and it felt like being wrapped in warm, comforting angel wings.

White Sands night

Others began to arrive and await the star talk for the evening program. The ranger arrived and as he was preparing for the program, dark clouds began to fill the sky. The wind started to blow harder and lightning began to fire from the clouds, accompanied by thunder, loud reminders of its power. The wind was so forceful it was challenging to stand without leaning into it. There was no safe choice other than retreating to the car. The program was postponed, but the show had been played out with perfection. No stars had been visible, but the light show before me displayed the power of the universe and our precarious place in it. It was a perfect ending to a perfect day.

Conversation with The Guys:

Pat: I feel a lot of confusion today. I am having experiences I can barely process and I have mixed feelings. It is hotter than I like, but there is something that makes me want to stay. I don't know what it is. I know I really like being in the Dunes. I feel so at peace.

Guys: Do you not yet understand what is going on? This is about listening to your inner knowing. There are things going on here that go deeper than you imagine. We are setting the stage for what is to come. All these things that seem like such little pieces are not so at all. They are important pieces of a larger plan. Allow for these things just to be what they are in each moment. Don't worry about what they mean or how they fit together at this time. You will know when need be. Now – gather the pieces. That is all you have to do right now.

Lesson from the day:
Become aware of your surroundings

We are constantly immersed in a soup of energy. We mix with the energy of the people around us. We share space with the objects and the Earth herself. All of these, including us, are made up of the energy that is everything in the universe. We are the same "stuff" as the stars, moon, planets, animals, rocks, and, oh yes, the person we're standing next to. The beggar on the street and the CEO of the largest corporation, the dictator and the oppressed, they are all the same. We are all made up of the same energy.

Here are some simple steps to notice and feel what is around you.

1. Look around and see what you see with your physical eyes.

2. Close your eyes and feel what you feel. You may feel the energy around you as a vibration, a memory, an emotion, or any number of different things that are unique to you. Do not judge; just notice. Examine whether it is what you thought it would be. Allow for a different perspective.

3. Whatever you feel will be interpreted through your own filters. If the feeling you have reminds you of something from your past experience, you will interpret it as that. Even though someone else will interpret it differently, you know what that energy means to you. Remember that AND be open to other possibilities.

4. Trust what you feel. This is your experience. You are accessing and interpreting the energy. Be true to you.

Day Five
Redefining Home

I chose to hike the dunes for the morning and it was a marvelous choice. Standing on the top of a gypsum dune in the morning as the sun rises in the sky is an experience to last a lifetime. There are no words to describe such beauty; it simply has to be experienced. Watching the light and shadows change on the diverse landscape was like watching a movie, a living picture, changing with each frame as it advanced.

Loneliness crept in and I was feeling very isolated. It was Saturday and the people I saw in the park were mostly couples or families with children. They were hiking and sliding down the sides of the dunes, laughing and playing together. It amplified how lonesome I was at that moment. As I hiked across the tops of the dunes, I knew I needed to connect with friends and family so I called home and talked as I sat in total stillness in this ethereal world.

The experience was unique in that hearing familiar voices from home did not lessen the loneliness. It felt weird, like home was no longer home. I was beginning to see that home is not a place. Home is something within us that we take with us wherever we go. I began to question what home was and could not come up with an answer. At that moment, home was on top of the dunes. As I drove, the car was my home. Each night, a motel room was my home. My world was changing rapidly.

The immensity of the landscape was overwhelming. The panorama could be viewed for three hundred and sixty degrees around me. I could stand and look around in any direction and see more of the same ethereal landscape. It was much like being in a dream. To the East and West were rows of mountain peaks, shining in the distance, like two rows of picket fences creating borders to the valley.

Many things come to awareness in the action of non-action, in the act of standing in stillness. Seeming to stand still does not mean we are not moving at light speed. We equate everything with the physical body, for that is what we are aware of in this medium of existence. We see, hear, touch, taste, and smell. We believe that these senses make up our reality. In fact, they have a large contribution to the experience, AND they are not all we possess. We also have senses we are either not aware of, or have forgotten how to use.

Intuition is one of those senses. Standing on that high perch and viewing the world from that perspective helped me to realize that we use few of our given talents, our innate power that is inbred in all of us. As much as the feeling of loneliness was in my awareness, there was also an awareness of something larger, bigger, more real than what we sense with our first five senses. There was a knowing that we are more than we believe we are. There is a connection to a larger whole. We are never alone, although we are often very private and seemingly separate from the rest of the world.

Our first five senses are associated with the physical body and have been used for survival since time began. I sensed that my life was unalterably changed, and that was coming from a place we can't categorize in a physical sense. This *knowing* is innate in all of us. We all have moments of experiencing things in a way we can't explain. We may call this strange and regard it as a fluke. I realized in that instant that these moments belong to all of us. They are not flukes of nature, but real abilities, a reality that is unseen, but non-the-less real. We are more than flesh and blood. We are more, MUCH MORE.

There were few people in the park that day, and watching

the natural inhabitants of that environment was a privilege. It was as if I had been allowed into a private viewing stand in a sacred, unknown world. It was fascinating to see how the residents of that environment reacted to humanity. One of them, a small, black beetle, stood on its head when I approached. It was telling me to go away. This small creature stood on its head and raised its posterior end to the sky. The message was loud and clear. I apologized for the intrusion into its world and left it alone as it regained its posture and went about its daily routine, once again walking in usual fashion.

Each thing in nature has its own way of protecting itself, including humans. I began to question what I do when I feel threatened, and realized there are many levels to this question. There are several things I might do on a physical level, but what about the underlying emotional levels? There are several ways we, as humans, stuff those things clear out of sight for self-protection.

None of us want to feel pain; that is why we choose to not deal with things that are painful to us. Sometimes we are aware of these things and consciously choose to put them aside. More often, we simply react to things and refuse to deal with them, not realizing that is what we did. We don't know, often until years later when a similar event occurs, that we stuffed these things far from our conscious awareness.

When we become aware of things we have hidden away, it is time to revisit them, choosing to let them out of their dark prison cells and shine light on them. This frees us, giving new meaning to the saying "And the truth shall set you free." These were the things coming into my awareness that day in that magical place. No longer would I find it acceptable to go about my life unconsciously, reacting without knowing why. It was time to start living my life with awareness, making conscious choices. This meant facing my fears when they arose, not putting them aside to deal with at a later time.

I hiked for hours, until the heat from the sun made it too difficult to continue. It was hard to leave, as much as the heat felt unbearable. The feeling of loneliness now gone, I did not want to leave this beauty, this solitude that connected me to the Universe. I thanked God, the Universe, and All That Is, for the experience and reluctantly moved on, knowing that some day I would return. This also now was home.

Up until this point, I had been feeling like nothing was happening. As I looked at the last few days, I was able to see more clearly. I was experiencing many events and these things seemed of little importance at the time they happened. Only in retrospect did they become important, and looking back allowed me to put all the small pieces into one whole. Each thing by itself makes little sense, yet when all the pieces are put together, a beautiful picture begins to emerge. It is not unlike the jigsaw puzzles that we build. Looking at one piece does not give us a picture.

With life it is nearly impossible to know what the finished picture will be, and having expectations of what the picture is, alters the experience. It is easy to miss the things that are happening in our lives when we look for a particular picture. We are too busy looking for one thing. If what we see is not what we expect, we miss what's there. If we know the finished picture will be a fruit and *expect* it to be an apple, and the pieces actually fit together to become an orange, we take the risk of missing what is really there AND being disappointed in the picture. My pieces, although early in the adventure, were beginning to fit together. Although I had no idea of what the finished picture would be, I could not have been happier to keep finding the pieces and see what would appear.

When we are unconcerned about what the destination will be, the journey becomes the joy and the focus, each event leading to the next in perfect harmony. This harmony, this synchronicity, is the way life was designed to work. Each thing we do brings us to the next thing. When we do what gives us the most joy, we are led to the next highest choice. When we do things we don't love, we are led to the next thing we don't love. The energy we put out is the energy we get back.

As I drove from this magnificent place, I took one last look around. Looking up at these dunes from the ground is a much different experience than viewing them from the top. It is like trying to see the forest when we are in the trees. It is impossible to get the whole picture and the details are magnified. It is much like life.

The afternoon proved to be equally interesting, although in a different way. I have long been fascinated with astronomy and space, so I took the time to visit the International Space Hall of Fame and museum. It is a four-story building, a golden cube, built on the hillside overlooking the valley. The view from the entrance is spectacular. It has a view of the valley floor, covered with white dunes, as far as the eye can see. Outside the entrance is a collection of space memorabilia, including a very impressive, full-sized model rocket. Inside are exhibits from the first rocket experiments to the Space Station and simulated Mars walk.

The afternoon was a lesson in synchronicity. A retired NASA employee was giving a fascinating talk on the Space Station. After the lecture, I felt a need to talk with this man, although I had no idea why. We talked of many things and he related many wonderful stories about the astronauts he had known and worked with. He was there at the conception of the space program and worked with the original astronauts. In the middle of this conversation, I remembered a book I had read about a scientist, now at NASA. I admired the man in the story and I asked the person I was speaking with if he had ever met the author of the book.

He became quite excited and told me the scientist in the book had taken over his job when he retired. He told me to wait while he went to his office and when he returned he had a paper in his hand. We talked for a little while longer and he looked puzzled, as if he was trying to decide something. He finally handed me the paper and said, "Would you like this"? It was an e-mail he received from this scientist, and had his address on it. I was stunned and amazed and took the paper.

I pondered this for a while, wondering why it was given to me. It took some time for the meaning to become clear. It was given to me as a physical reminder of synchronicity. When I was ready to ask the question, the exact right person was there to answer it. Had I not been open to following up on my intuitions, I would not have had that interaction. Life is a perfect orchestration, written by master composers and played out by each and every one of us in perfect harmony.

First I was drawn to talk to the man who gave the lecture. It was no mystery that I remembered the book when I was speaking with him. It was not a mystery that his job had been filled by the scientist. It was no mystery that he just "happened to have" that e-mail. It was no mystery that he gave it to me. All was synchronicity, perfect harmony in action, all played out at that moment so I could see it.

As I left there and returned to my "home" for the night, I was once again filled with more questions than answers, but now they became a comfort. We never have all the answers. Each answer will bring another question and each pursuit of answers to those questions will bring us to the next. It is all in perfect order and sequence. Ahhhh, how perfect this universe.

That night I was in need of rest, not because I was physically tired, but I needed time to sit back and let everything sink in. I would be leaving Alamagordo in the morning and had no idea what direction I would be heading. I was thinking about going south to Las Cruces, and then heading east to Tucson, but knew that I would wait until morning and see what felt right. As had become my morning ritual, I would sit in silence and see what my next move would be.

Conversation with The Guys:

Pat: I'm leaving tomorrow and have no idea what direction to go in.

Guys: Follow your nose. It has worked well for you all your life and you are now ready to step it up a notch. Feel the direction you are to go in. If you miss it, we will tell you, as we did to get you to go through Ruidoso. We told you that you will not miss things; we will not let you. You are doing well.

Pat: I had an expectation of meeting someone, a teacher of some sort, in the desert and that has not happened. I also know it has only been 5 days, AND it may not happen at all. That is the trouble with expectations. I thought I came without any and I was wrong.

Guys: You are working with human capabilities, in the physical sense; this tends to complicate things from an energy standpoint. This is not something you are doing wrong, just that you are working with what you have known. Do not judge yourself.

Pat: When I think about going home I don't know what I'll do when I get there. I have a feeling things can never be the same after this. I don't know what has changed, but it feels like I am shifting somehow.

Guys: Time, give yourself time to do this journey. You are taking pieces and trying to make them be the whole. You don't have enough pieces yet to do that. Do you understand?

Pat: Yes. I am being impatient and trying to do the impossible. I will remind myself to be patient when I am feeling lost and alone.

Guys: Let it go. See all the things that you do from habit and ritual and let them go. This is about noticing and changing. Awareness. Choice. You will be learning much about yourself and changing many things that no longer fit. Do not look for such big things to happen. Take the small pieces and know that they will fit into a larger one. You are putting the cart before the horse.

Pat: Yes, I am expecting too much.

Guys: NO. Expect miracles Dear Heart, but do not judge the miracles or look for them in any particular place. Accept all that happens as miracle. Know this. Accept this with love. Rest and relax now. Tomorrow is another day and we will be with you in the driver's seat, and the back seat, and the under seat and over seat. Feel us. We are there and will never, not be.

Lesson from the day: Home is not a place

Home has as many definitions as the people defining them. It is important to each and every one of us to know what that is to us. The reason it is so important is that if we don't know what defines home for us, we will spend the rest of our lives trying to find something that is outside of ourselves. It will never be found for it lives within us. It is also important to know that home changes in each moment. What is home in one moment may not be the same in the next AND that is OK. It is perfect.

To find home you have to start in your own heart and here are a few things that may help you get there.

1. Home is NOT a place – it is a feeling, a knowing deep inside yourself.

2. Feel that place inside where you feel peace. Is that peace still with you in your surroundings?

3. If you are not comfortable and at peace with a person, place or thing, you are not home.

4. When you are feeling like you could stay where you are forever, you are.

When in doubt – go back to that quiet place in your heart and feel if it represents your true self.

Day Six
Healing Mother Earth

Once again, my idea of the best way to go was not to become reality. As I sat in silence and connected with my internal guidance, the name Magdelena keep running through my consciousness and I knew I had to go north, not south. I took the time to treat myself to a leisurely breakfast, as I was unsure how long it would be before I could do so again. I had no idea where I was going except north, toward Magdelena. I trusted this would be perfect.

I was becoming comfortable driving without a map. I simply put my hands on the steering wheel and told God, The Guys, they could lead me where I needed to go. When I approached a road that seemed like the best one, I would simply feel a need to turn into it, or hear that inner voice that reaffirmed it. At times I would just find myself turning the wheel, as if someone reached down and took my hands and did it for me. You might say the journey was leading me, opening doors in front of me, instead of my trying to make it happen the way I thought it should.

The glistening, white valley floor sped by the windows as I glided silently northward. Sage and small shrubs grew along the roadway, creating splotches of color and adding contrast to the white gypsum. Train tracks ran the length of the valley, adding diversity. The alternate landing site for the Space Shuttle was nearby and miles of quiet wonder lay ahead. Soft clouds drifted silently overhead, like sentinels, keeping watch over my journey.

The energy in the valley felt strangely absent in places,

as if a great death had occurred. I was drawn to pull over in a few places and visualize light columns opening up over the valley, renewing Mother Earth with the energy of love and light. There was a feeling of reverence associated with this experience. I felt honored and privileged to be a part of this grand plan.

Approaching the northern part of the valley brought with it more wonders as white was replaced with black. I had entered what is called "The Malpais", a huge lava bed that covers the northern valley floor. If I had been able to see this from above, I imagine it would have looked like an elongated basin, one end filled with salt and the other end with pepper. My perspective was much smaller however; I could not see the forest for the trees, and I was enjoying the contrast as I moved from white to black.

There is a park with boardwalks, built to accommodate visitors who want to walk through this unique landscape. Huge formations of lava cover the ground and sporadic growths of vegetation spring from them at random. It is truly a wondrous sight, to see life proliferating from what appears to be uninhabitable matter. It creates an eerie landscape and I found it uniquely quiet, even when filled with visitors.

I was once again challenged to examine my beliefs, this time about life itself. How did these plants grow? Where did they come from? What nurtured them and enabled their continued existence? What nurtures us? How do we, as humans, continue our existence, against seemingly insurmountable odds? In comparison, the vegetation seemed to shout its triumph. The plants seemed aware only of life, taking nourishment from the meager environment and growing toward the sun in perfect harmony within their world. Can we do the same?

I started to look at the times I have complained because things were not as I had hoped, had felt sorry for not having more, and I felt humbled by these courageous plants. We have so much, and yet we seldom see it, for we are looking for something outside ourselves. These plants had no such cares. I imagine if I asked these plants what they lived for they would say, "to experience life and to grow." A simple answer, for they have no self-awareness; they are one with the Universe.

What do we do with our self-awareness? Do we use it to grow? Is life that simple? I believe we could take a lesson from the plants I witnessed in their miraculous glory that day. They know nothing of hate, borders, separation, prejudice, greed, or any other thing we create when we forget we are one with the Universe. They do not compete with their neighbor to grow faster, get there first, have the most water, or be the fairest of all. They simply **are** and, I imagine, feel joy at the simplicity of life.

Life is simple. It is not always easy, but it is definitely simple. When we find ourselves caught up in the trauma/drama, the confusion, the story, we are in the wrong place. It is time to step back, take a deep breath, and reevaluate our position. These plants reminded me to keep my focus on the simplicity of life and to be grateful for all the basic, simple things I find within. It is only when I look outside myself that I find reason for unhappiness and conflict.

I drove in silence, contemplating the wisdom of the Universe. I was not paying full attention to my surroundings when I passed a road with a sign that said Stallion Gate, White Sands Missile Range. Shortly after passing this entrance, I found myself doing a U-turn and going back to that road. It was one of those times the hands reached down and turned the wheel for me. Once again I was not sure why, as the road led through a military installation. I became more anxious as I drove, but was drawn forward in spite of myself.

A feeling of fear crept in as the road continued through the desert. There was an eerie feel to the site and part of me wanted to turn around and leave. It seemed like the road would go on forever and finally I came to a gated checkpoint with a soldier standing guard. I parked the car, took a deep breath, to steady myself and gain courage, and walked toward the guard. I was not sure why, but I asked him if the Trinity Site was nearby; I had a feeling it was. He got very excited. He took me by the hand and brought me around the checkpoint to where I could see beyond. He then pointed out a barren piece of hollowed out earth in the distance and told me this was a crater, caused by the atomic bomb. I had driven to the exact site where the bomb was tested on July 16, 1945.

Tours are held twice a year for those who want to enter the area and see the test site from a closer perspective. Part of me wondered why anyone would want to do that and part of me knew that this wound could be healed if enough well intentioned individuals brought love to it. At that present moment however, I just wanted to get in my car and drive away as quickly as I could. I wanted to run from this place like a dog with its tail on fire.

I felt like I had ice in my veins and yet I was mesmerized by the excitement in this young man's voice. He was thrilled to be there, and I was devastated. He was so excited about being where history took place and I was appalled at the reason for this history. He told me of a bomb fragment about the size of a thermos that was found a couple years ago at the site. They tried to blow it up without success. It was encased in cement and put in a park in Socorro, a town nearby. He repeated this a few times and I knew I would be following up on that clue. I had been given another piece in my puzzle.

As I drove back out the long entrance road I turned to look at the crater and was overwhelmed by the horrendous energy in the area. Once again I was drawn to open a light column, this time directly over the crater. I have since heard that there are groups of like-minded people like myself who are now going to these areas to do exactly that. I could not be more thrilled. As more and more people add love and light to such areas, Mother Earth will be healed. It may sound strange, but she sustains wounds, just as we do, and heals in a similar manner.

Once again on the main road, I saw without seeing, my heart filled with emotion. The sadness and grief of the land was overwhelming, as if calling from some unknown grave. At the same time, there was a feeling of renewed energy, the twinkling of a birth. I was beginning to see the power we all hold within our grasp. That power is love and when we share that love with the Universe, miracles begin to happen. Adding light and love with the intention of healing creates miracles beyond our wildest dreams and imagination.

Nelson Mandela once said that we are not afraid of being inadequate, that we fear our power and are more afraid of our light than our darkness. I believe he was correct. We hold the power of the Universe within our grasp and deny we have it. Jesus told us we could do what He did and more and we say that is not what He meant. Buddha and other great teachers have had similar teachings. It is time to look within and accept our own divinity, our own connection to God. We can change the world.

The people in Socorro were quietly going about their business and helpful when I asked for directions to the park. I had been told the cement container for the bomb fragment would be found at the base of a WWII canon. If it had not been for the canon, I would never have found the container. There were holes in the cement where it appeared a marker had been placed and removed. Only a nondescript hunk of cement remained, lying quietly at the base of this implement of war.

Near this encasement was a memorial to the Vietnam

Veterans. It was in the shape of a pyramid and was an understated, yet awesome sight. I had gone to this park on a quest to find a bomb encasement from a weapon of mass destruction created in 1945, and stood enthralled, in front of a very different object, although created because of a similar circumstance. War. I wondered why I had been drawn to this spot. I was magnetized to the pyramid, which shone brightly in the sparkling sun.

Although there are no mistakes in this Universe, it is not always apparent why things happen as they do. Some things make immediate sense and there is no question of the why. Some things take months or years to understand and I was beginning to see that some things might never be understood. Some things we need to do on faith, knowing the reason will show itself when and where it is needed.

What we expect is not always what we find. Perhaps the reason I was led there was not to find the encasement, but that's what it took to get me there. Sometimes we are sent in a direction and when we go there we find something different than we thought we would find, yet better and more perfect for us at the time. Maybe I needed to go there to see that pyramid, or for someone else, perhaps someone who is reading these words. Perhaps it was for me to see the deeper meaning of things and more deeply question my beliefs. I may never know.

These reminders of war brought more questions to the surface. How many beings have been killed in the name of peace? Do peace and killing go together? We kill for God, for Love, and for Peace. What is wrong with this picture? We have been fooling ourselves into believing this can be true. Veterans of WWII will probably tell you they were there fighting for peace. Veterans of Vietnam may tell you something different. The world is changing. When we find love in our hearts, we begin to question old beliefs. When we realize we are all connected, we become less willing to cause harm to another. This is love.

With these things in mind, I drove in peaceful contemplation. The landscape changed from a desert vista to a mountain wonderland as I approached Magdelena, in the dry plains of San Agustin. Mountain peaks surrounded me, stretching to the sky like fingers reaching to touch the heavens. It was a breathtaking sight. It looked as if God reached down into the mountains and set a flat valley, almost at the top of the peaks.

About a half-hour past Magdelena, at an altitude of 7000 feet, I came upon rows of radio telescopes in the shape of a flattened Y, spreading across the flat plain. If anyone saw the movie *Contact,* they saw this sight, as this is where part of the movie was filmed. It is the National Radio Astronomy Observatory, or the VLA, and is a spectacular sight. It is the world's most powerful telescope. It is not one large structure but an array of 27 antennas, which are connected electronically to synthesize a single radio telescope 20 miles in diameter.

The view of these dish telescopes is awesome from a distance, and from a closer perspective, the sheer size of them is stunning. There was a self-guided tour that was not to be missed and I got to see first-hand how the universe is mapped. Seeing radio photographs of The Milky way, The Orion Nebula, the birth of a star, a supernova remnant, a whirlpool galaxy, radio galaxies and normal galaxies is humbling beyond words.

Earth, as we see it from our perspective, is huge. It is our home and the center of our personal universe. What about all the things we see out there in space? What about the things we are yet unable to see with our present technology and equipment? These questions filled my awareness and brought me to places yet unknown or unremembered. Was I looking at worlds that held beings such as us, or not like us, who see their world as the center of their universe? Was I viewing worlds of other civilizations, yet unable to see them, as they would be unable to see us from this distance? The questions abounded.

Once again I found myself reluctant to leave where I was. It was nearing late afternoon and I was unsure of any place ahead that had lodging for the night. I was heading west and the guard at the VLA knew of no accommodations anywhere nearby. It was no mistake then that I met a couple from Texas, who had at one time lived a few miles from me in Connecticut. We shared a history of mutual places and had a wonderful conversation. The woman had arthritis and they told me they were heading south, through the mountains, to a place called Truth or Consequences. They go there often to enjoy the hot springs and baths. They told me, three times, the route they would be taking and highly recommended it, saying it would be a highlight of my day. It felt right, so I followed their advice. I was not disappointed.

Had I not known where I was, I would have imagined myself to be in an alpine meadow, perhaps in Switzerland. Ahead stretched miles of meadow and mountain. To my surprise, the road was dirt. I was still in high plains, surrounded by mountain peaks and the road became increasingly hilly. The sky blackened and bolts of lightning lit the darkness in the distance. I was in the middle of what seemed like nowhere and I felt the pangs of fear creep in once again. What would I do if the car broke down? Who would ever find me? Taking a deep breath, I connected to the peace and serenity of the world within. The outer world in my visual field grew in its beauty to unimaginable proportions.

Forty miles of dirt road seemed to float through this valley like a magic carpet in a fairy tale world. In places, vines of melons grew across the road and wild white roses filled the roadside. Cows grazed freely on the roadside and took time to check out the few cars that visited their home. I discovered that a calf could turn around, seemingly in mid-air. Its mother stood by the side of the road, blocking its view of my approach. Startled from seeing the car as it stepped from behind its mother, the little thing appeared to jump up, turn in mid-air and land on the ground, going in the opposite direction. Whether it did or it simply appeared that way is still a mystery, but it took no time making its departure from the roadside. It was a bit of comic relief to brighten the spirit and dissolve the fear, another gift of the Universe, a gift from God.

The road to Truth or Consequences

Rain splattered on the windshield, becoming heavy at times and turning the dust into mud. The white car escorting me on my journey was slowly turning black. There were times I wondered if I was in the right place, doing the right thing. I continued the journey, choosing to trust this was perfect and choosing to find joy in the moment. We think that happiness or joy is a result of our interactions with our environment, but we choose it in each moment, or we don't. We can choose to be joyful with our lives, or choose to be fearful and unhappy. It is always, all ways, our choice. Eventually the dirt road became pavement and signs of civilization began to emerge. I was exhausted from the events of the day and the challenging drive, but reached Truth or Consequences with joy in my heart.

The town is named such because of the TV show of the same name. Ralph Edwards, the moderator of the show, had promised many things to any town that took on the name, and so this town got its name. There is a park named Ralph Edwards Riverside Park, and the town is a tourist Mecca, due to the Hot Springs, baths, and nearby lakes. It is an interesting experience to see large lakes with huge marinas in the middle of the desert. The contrast is mind-boggling.

It was Sunday and the baths I was told to look for seemed not to be open. If they were, I was too tired to notice and decided to rest for the evening. So many things had happened in just a few days that I was unable to process the information. I was finding that as we experience events, we do not always immediately integrate what is happening into our awareness. It sometimes takes months, if not years, to absorb all the information and experience.

I started out in the morning, expecting to go south and ended up making a 300-mile loop, ending up on the other side of the mountains I viewed from Alamagordo. I sat on Gypsum dunes the day before and watched the East side of the same mountain I was now looking at from the West. It seemed I could forget about planning any part of this adventure. I was learning to trust in the perfection of the Universe and the synchronicity of all things. Although it was challenging to let go of all control, I knew I would be led exactly where I needed to go. Such it would be with this adventure, as it would become in my life.

Conversation with The Guys:

Pat: Today was certainly interesting. I keep being led around these mountain chains. Before I came out here I was asked to know them, and now I am being led back and forth around them. I've studied them from the maps, talked to people who live here, seen them from the air and now I'm in them. Why?

Guys: Know this; it is **paramount** *that you know this terrain. This may not become evident to you for some time, but there will be a day when you look back at this and know, without any doubt, why you have come to do this. Please accept this as an explanation, for it is the best we can do at this moment in time.*

Pat: OK. I choose to trust. My phone will not hold a charge for a whole day and I am wondering if you are getting me ready to be out of contact, kind of an easing into a separation from 3-D. It seems like each day I become more alone. It was really strange talking with my husband today. It was so surreal. It feels strange.

Guys: Know this Dear Heart; there are many things that will be changing in your life soon. This is just a preparation for those things to happen. What that will be and in what way it will play out depends on many things. You will know more as time passes. Decisions will be made from the choices that will "pop up." You are learning how to live in this manner. This is also a lesson in living completely in synchronicity. You are learning to follow the clues, the leads that are given. We have been putting them in front of you and you are doing well.

Lesson from the day: Earth Needs Healing Too

We tend to think of healing as something reserved for people or perhaps the animal kingdom. We seldom apply the concept to Earth herself. We have, for the most part, forgotten that she is a living, breathing being. She breathes air through her trees and her waters wave and flow with the moon tides. She is in perfect harmony with the universe around her.

It is we who alter that balance. We have ripped her apart, blown her up, stripped her of every resource and removed the very core of her being. We cut down the trees, pollute the water and disrespect every aspect of her existence. She is like us. We get cut, we bleed. We get hurt, we feel pain. Is there something we can do to change this? Yes.

1. Recognize that she is the same energy that you are. You are one.

2. Know that if you destroy her, you destroy yourself and greatly decrease your chance of survival.

3. Send love and healing thoughts to her at all times.

4. Imagine her as your mother or daughter and treat her with respect.

5. Create sanctuaries where people can commune with her. Play. Share your love.

6. Hug a tree. Clean a beach. Stop litter.

7. Protect her from harm. Speak up to stop acts of destruction and desecration of her.

Day Seven
Seeing from a Different Perspective

The San Andres Mountains, reverently gazed upon from the dunes a few days earlier at sunset were no less spectacular from the other side at sunrise as the sun rose up and over them, radiating and back-lighting them like sparkling crystal around dark, gloved fingers. The effect was stunning. The Rio Grande River meandered down the valley at the base of this chain of mountains, keeping them company in their stationary place in our world.

How many things in our world seem so solid, so steadfast and secure? These mountains conveyed a feeling of permanence in an ever-changing world. If we could view these same mountains in a time-lapse photograph, over eons, we would see them grow from flat land to high peaks. We do not have the luxury of this perspective however, and see them as solid and stationary.

In our physical world, perspective is everything. Things are seldom what they seem on the surface. Just as these mountains change with time, so do we. What a wonderful gift it was to see this perspective shining through the crystal glow, in the wonder of that moment. How like these mountains we are!

As I passed this scene, I noticed a road to my right and felt a need to go in that direction. The road was straight and the terrain flat for miles on end. Passing a small farm store, I stopped to browse and met the owner, a wonderful man of Mexican descent, who told me stories of his farm and how he prepares his spices. The world is filled with wonderful people and he reminded me how important it is to use every opportunity to connect with them. There is so much we can learn if we only extend a hand to another.

I had been feeling for a few days that I was hanging onto something, that there was an emotional issue I was not letting go of. I had no idea what it was so I asked God, The Guys, to help me find it and to give me clarity on this issue. Be careful what you ask for!

I began to experience intense pain in my upper right abdomen. I decided to visualize the area in my mind and see if I could tell what was causing the pain. I focused on the area and to my surprise, I saw a young Native American girl, about 5 years old. She was attached with a cord to the area around Alamagordo. She was hanging on for dear life and digging in her heels like a mule. She told me I was trying to rip her away from her home again.

I could see her in the mountains in Mescalero and knew it was connected to the feeling that I had been there before, although I had no idea what it meant. She was unwilling to let go and the pain increased. She was terrified and wanted me to go back to that area. I told her I could not, but I would return at a later date and see if I could resolve this problem. She was reluctantly agreeable. I asked God for help in resolving this. The pain disappeared!

We are multidimensional beings and are connected to many things. Some call this past life, or alternate life experience. Some of you will find nothing strange about this; others of you will think it odd or unbelievable. Whatever it is, there is a connection to many things we cannot explain. Where it comes from, where it originates is up for interpretation. I only ask when you experience these things, that you keep an open mind and acknowledge the experience without judgment. We are more than we imagine ourselves to be.

The road I was on turned out to be a great shortcut to the

highway in Arizona, the one I had originally planned to take the day before. This would lead me to Tucson as I had hoped. The terrain changed from flat to hilly and rocky. Giant spires of rock towered toward the sky like steeples on ancient Gothic cathedrals. Deep crevasses opened up and ravines lined the roadside interspersed with these rocky formations. All were painted in earth colors of reds and browns. The road wound over, around, and through these formations, creating passage for weary travelers such as I.

Tucson is a sprawling city, set in the shelter of the surrounding mountains. It was hotter than it had been in New Mexico and I made doubly sure there was an adequate supply of water in the car at all times. After getting settled and taking a moment to refocus and rebalance, I chose to visit Saguaro National Park.

Each place I had been was a small universe in itself. Each was different and equally inspiring. This was to be yet another in a series of magical places. The narrow road wound like a serpent through miles of hilly terrain, each hill covered with saguaro cacti. Some were as tall as fifty feet and weighed up to eight tons. Considering it takes up to seventy-five years for the first arm to grow, the sheer age and endurance they display is astounding. Some of them are more than one hundred and fifty years old.

I thought about what has happened in the last one hundred and fifty years and was beyond words. Some of these were born when Lincoln was president. They saw the advent of the automobile and men walking on the moon. The technology developed in their years on this earth is beyond precedent. They are living memorials to a history we have only read about. The concept was overwhelming.

Standing in the midst of such earthly elders is an awesome experience. To stand in silence and feel the energy of such life

Hiking Saguaro National Park

is not to be missed. Taking advantage of the opportunity, I donned my hiking gear and walked out among these wondrous creations. Many other types of cacti grow among these giants and all were beautiful. I stood and breathed in the beauty around me, filling me with the love of the Universe.

I felt soothed, like a newborn held in the loving arms of its mother, and realized that was not far from the truth. Mother Earth was named "Mother" for a reason. She is our mother in many ways. She holds the collective energy of all who live upon her. She nurtures us with her offspring. The food grown from her soil gives us health-giving nutrients. The water from her body gives us life. Her trees give us not only shelter, but yet the air we breathe.

We need to see what we are doing to our collective mother, our birthright, and we must make new choices if we would like her to continue to nourish us, to protect us. We are in this together. What we give out we will get back.

This she reminded me of as I absorbed her energy and shared her love in this universe. I felt renewed and was once again ready to move along on my adventure. As I drove, slowly meandering through the hills and valleys of this wondrous place, I thanked God for my many blessings. It is easy in our every day lives to forget to be grateful. I was discovering that this is prayer.

We have thought of prayer as an asking for something, a request for what we believe we want or need. I found, in those precious moments, that prayer is giving thanks for what we know we already have. What we pray for is given before we ask. It is a simple knowing this is true that opens the energy to flow. From there all things are possible. Prayers are always, all ways answered. We can only believe they are not answered when the answer is not what we told God we wanted. If we pray for an apple and receive a pear, we may see it was answered, or believe it was not.

It was getting late in the day, fatigue was setting in and the heat was stifling. As I approached the city I once again tried to use the map and got hopelessly lost. In the heat of the moment, I had unconsciously chosen not to trust the larger plan to unfold exactly as it is meant to, in perfect harmony. As I became frustrated, I realized I had made that choice and stopped for directions. I was one block from my motel and going in circles. I still had much to learn.

Conversation with The Guys:

Pat: I feel like a character in one of James Redfield's books.

Guys: It is so, for that is what you are learning to do. You are learning to trust the larger plan to unfold exactly as it is supposed to, for precise reasons. You now see that there will always be someone, or something there to guide you. You will have exactly what you need, exactly when you need it. It is perfect.

*Tomorrow will be another day of fun and excitement for you. **Make** each day, each moment, fun and exciting. You are the master of your destiny, the captain of your soul. You are now learning to live 3-D from a higher perspective. You are **living** it. How does that feel?*

Pat: Wonderful. It's a whole new way of doing things. It's a lot easier just trusting than having to plan things out and try to make them happen. I'm using the map very little and ending up just where I need to be. When I forget that I get lost.

Guys: And so it is. You will be doing more of this in the next few weeks of your time. We have many surprises in store for you. Do not be discouraged that nothing will happen. More is happening than you can possibly imagine. You will never be the same again My Dear One, never the same again.

Lesson from the day: Perspective

Perspective determines our experience of the world. Ten people will view something from ten different angles and perspectives and so their experience will be different. If I view a tree from one side and you see it from the other, we will see something very different. Is it the same tree? Yes, but our experience of it is not.

It's easy to get caught up in thinking what we see is the only correct view. This comes from a belief that things have to be this OR that. In truth, they are this AND that. Both views are correct and perfect for each person. Here are a few simple steps to look clearly and open to a larger understanding.

1. Notice what you notice. Take in the details from your present viewing point.

2. Look from another perspective. A tree on the sunny side is bright. The other side is dark.

3. Discuss what you see with others who see from their own perspective.

4. Remember that what you see is only a small part of the whole.

5. It takes all the views together to complete a whole picture.

6. Be willing to accept each person's perspective as valid. Your view is no more real or important than that of every other person viewing the same thing.

Day Eight
A larger view of the Universe

The morning dawned with a renewed brilliance, bringing joy and anticipation to yet another wonderful day. The road changed from multi-lane with a mass of street signs and traffic lights to a two-lane road slicing through an open, flat desert, this one painted in shades of ochre and brown with green shrubs dotting the scene. Mountains in the distance conveyed strength to the scene and a sense of protection. They loomed ever closer and closer as the desert slid by.

I was crossing the Sonoran Desert, 56 miles through the Coyote Mountains Wilderness, and approaching the Quinlan Mountains and Kitt Peak National Observatory. Seeing the first telescope on the peak from the desert floor was a breathtaking sight. The observatory is on the Tohono O'odham Reservation and on top of Kitt Peak, at an elevation of 6,875 feet. Driving the twelve miles of road up the mountain to the observatory was an adventure in itself.

The road snaked up the mountain like a coiled, frightened serpent, holding onto the mountainside for its very life. The view was spectacular and I found I was often holding my breath as I drove. The drop off from the road was thousands of feet in many places. I needed to remind myself to breathe – often. I thanked God that I was rarely afraid of heights and was able to continue.

The observatory is home to twenty-two optical and two radio telescopes and is associated with dozens of astronomical research institutions. It has the world's largest collection of optical telescopes and houses the world's largest solar telescope. I was, for the third time in just a few days, gazing at the sky, seeing other worlds from a magnified perspective. As I did the self-guided tour of the facility, I wondered why I was being guided to observe such celestial wonder.

As I was listening to a lecture at one of the telescopes, I kept hearing The Guys whispering in my ear, hearing that inner voice that was becoming so familiar. I was told to leave where I was and go to a different telescope. I questioned the voice and stayed where I was, enjoying the lecture. The voice became louder, more insistent, and I felt the need to listen. I slipped silently out.

There was a large hill leading up to the telescope I was being led to and it looked like an easy walk. I had not taken the altitude into consideration. What seemed like a short walk, turned into another adventure. Instead of rushing to the destination, I needed to stop and rest from time to time. I chose to go slower and enjoy the sights along the way, which brought treasures of its own.

There was a telescope on the path, which was not open to the public. It was being repaired and a group of young women "happened" to be walking by. It was being utilized at the time by the college that these girls attended. Because of that, they were admitted to the building and given a tour. As I stopped and talked with these women, they told me this story and related that it was a "serendipitous" occurrence. It was wonderful seeing others realize that things are synchronous. It was yet one more affirmation of the harmony of the Universe.

I wondered why I had been sent to that particular telescope. It was a spectacular scientific marvel, but there was no one there and nothing I found of particular interest. I headed back toward the Center and stopped for a drink at the bottom the hill. A man stepped from one of the buildings and joined me. He was a scientist, an astronomer studying Gamma Ray Bursts. As we walked up the hill housing the Visitor Center, he gave me a brief description of what they are and I felt the excitement with which he viewed them. He said they were the most powerful things in the universe, at least ten times more powerful than Solar Flares.

It was a wonderful treat. I was given, on that short walk, a lesson I would never have gotten anywhere else. His excitement was infectious and I found myself wishing I were an astronomer also, looking for answers to our Universal history and heritage. I still don't know why it was important for me to have had that lesson, but I have no doubt that I was sent there to meet him. It felt perfect and I felt like I had known that young man for a lifetime, an old friend revisited.

The Visitor Center contained a gift shop with many wonderful things, some made by the Tohono O'odham tribe, an agreement made for having the observatory on their land. There was also a wonderful collection of books for sale and one of them, *Einstein's Universe*, by Nigel Calder, seemed to "jump off the shelf" at me. It remains one of my favorites to this day.

The universe is a magnificent sight. How often I had stared at the sky, looking but not seeing. We seem to spend our lives looking at most things without really seeing them. We need to take the time to see what is in front of us, to look with more than our physical eyes. We need to see with our eyes AND feel what is there. We need to question what we are curious about, to accept what feels right and to reject what does not.

Questioning will bring us information, answers, but will not give us wisdom. Information brings us knowledge and will guide us to make informed decisions. Wisdom comes from a place unseen, a deeper place within our being. This connection to an all-knowing consciousness, or God, is inherent in all of us and is accessed by going within. When we go within we will not go without!

Leaving the mountain was an opportunity to see the world from yet one more perspective. The view from that height was breathtaking and would have stayed as a living memory in my life, even if it had not been for the storm that I saw approaching. We seldom see a storm from above the clouds. We are usually experiencing them from the perspective of a participant.

As I watched, dark clouds swept across the desert toward the mountains, a sheet of white rain below them, like white linen hanging on a clothesline. Around the storm there was nothing but sunshine and clear sky. I began to see how my own life had often felt like that. Sometimes things would seem sunny and clear and suddenly a dark cloud would surround me, leaving a feeling of doom and gloom.

Kitt Peak storm

I found that the dark feelings would persist as long as I fought them and gave energy to their arrival. When I allowed them to simply move through and refused to give in to the fear they brought, they were gone rather quickly. I watched as this storm moved through, unimpeded. It moved quite fast and was gone as quickly as it came. How like life the world around us is. What a perfect mirror!

I stopped at a small convenience store in the Coyote Wilderness area and had the opportunity of speaking with a wonderful woman in charge of the craft section. She was of Tohono O'odham descent and had several local crafts on display. There was a section of Sweet Grass Baskets she considered of lesser quality, perhaps done by the younger children who were learning the art. I fell in love with one of them. It was a small basket, about five inches in diameter and not quite symmetrical, therefore considered not as valuable as the others.

I bought this basket because it reminded me of our human qualities here on Earth. We are all beautiful, and each of us has what we call our imperfections. Often we believe that these imperfections take away from our beauty and make us less valuable. I disagree. I have this basket on my desk so I am reminded daily that our beauty is always evident. The imperfections do not take away from that beauty, but enhance it. Each thing adds to our uniqueness and helps make us who we are.

This got me thinking once again as I drove back through this beautiful country. How often had I put myself down for not being perfect? At times I still do. I have striven for perfection my whole life. One of my daughters once called me driven. No wonder my back had become so rigid. Things were starting to make sense. I was beginning to see how I had designed my life around what I *believed* I should be, instead of what was in my heart.

I think we all do that to some extent. We have a picture of what we think we should be and we do all we can to accomplish that. When we are not successful in the attempt, we believe we failed. That leaves two things to overcome – the frustration of not being what we wanted to be, and the added weight of failure. In actuality, we set ourselves up for failure when we try to be what we are not.

When we do what does not give us joy, we are doomed to be less than successful. Even if we manage to succeed, it will be an empty victory if we are not happy being who we are, doing what we don't love. It is a self-perpetuating cycle, keeping us locked in the every day routine, living without joy. The world may view us as successful, but at what cost to us?

I knew I would no longer choose to live my life by what the world valued as success. I would follow my heart, even if it seemed like an unpopular decision to those around me. It was time I lived from my own heart. To do that I had to accept what was really in my heart, not what I wanted to find there. I could no longer deny my true feelings or be what I was not. I knew the days ahead would bring more change than I could imagine. Even that was grossly understated.

It was becoming my custom to keep food in the cooler for most of my meals. When travelling like this, I found it easier to keep things like cereal and non-perishables for a quick, economical breakfast, and bread and peanut butter, etc, for quick lunches. Often, I would find myself in the desert at mealtimes, with no place for miles to get food. If there was a market nearby, a fresh salad was a wonderful treat for dinner when I was too tired to go out.

That afternoon I chose to do some shopping. I was in need of a break. Coming back to the motel, I decided to swim in the pool and watch the children. This time it was a different surprise. The water in the pool was approximately 95 degrees. If any of you have ever tried to swim in very warm water, I will tell you it is a unique experience. It is challenging to do any serious exercising; laps were out of the question.

Children were coming to the pool and excitedly jumping in. The looks on their faces added the humor I needed to end my day. It was wonderful to see the surprise and pure excitement on their faces as they entered the hot water. They laughed, splashed, and giggled, enticing their parents to explore this unique experience. They had not a care in the world, it was only the adults who reacted with something less than approval. It once again reinforced my belief that we must become as little children, finding pure joy in every thing we do, with every thing we encounter.

Conversation with The Guys:

Pat: When you told me to go to the 4 meter telescope and I didn't listen at first, what happened? I finally left in the middle of the tour and went there and it seemed like nothing happened. Then I met that wonderful young scientist who gave me a science lesson on Gamma Ray Bursts. Was that why you sent me to that telescope? Was that what I went for?

Guys: Yes, yes and yes. You altered the timing slightly, but all worked out perfectly.

Pat: Why was it important for me to hear that?

Guys: It is not important to know at this time. There are many things happening that will make no sense. We told you this before. Just let it be what it is. There will come a day when some of these things will come to your awareness and you will say "Oh, now I know why that happened." Others you may never understand and that is OK too. Just know there is a reason.

Pat: So I did not mess anything up by not listening at first?

Guys: No, you just altered the timing slightly. We will not allow you to miss anything.

Pat: What is the tremendous pull I feel for the area between Roswell and Alamagordo? I feel sooooooooooooo attached to that whole area. I feel like going back and wonder if I missed something and need to go back.

Guys: Either way is OK. There is more you will be doing and seeing in NM. Know that there is a connection that goes beyond logic. You are not wrong to be where you are. There is just more to do there at some time. You were correct in intuiting the past connection. It is very strong and will continue to draw you there.

Pat: Would it be more beneficial to just let go of the connection? It actually hurt to leave.

Guys: It is OK. Letting go of the things that create a negative energy bandlink is beneficial. Keeping the love and the wisdom is very powerful and will be a tremendous connection for you in the future. You will become clearer on this soon.

Lesson from the day: Synchronicity

Everything in life is connected, just as we are connected to everything in life. It is sometimes called the circle of life. Because we are living in a world that is experienced as separation, it seems like each thing is random. When we look at it from the perspective of a circle, we can see how all things are connected and one thing leads to another, in perfect harmony. The experience at Kitt Peak shows how this works.

When we pay attention and follow our inner feelings, we are led perfectly. When we do not, we alter the timing or sequence of events. It does not mean we will not end up with the same lesson, but the experience will be quite different. There is nothing wrong with either, but following a conscious path of connection feels much more comfortable than the roller coaster ups and downs of separation.

Think of it as jumping from one place in the circle to the other side, then back to another spot and so forth. Then think of moving from one place in the circle to a place that is connected in either direction. You will eventually get to the other side and the journey will be easier and smoother.

Here are a few things to remember to help you recognize the signposts along the way that lead you in a smoothly orchestrated dance with life.

1. Notice what you notice. Look around; see where you are.

2. Was there something you experienced in your "past" that influenced you being there?

3. If you are sensing there is somewhere to go from where you are, do so if possible.

4. Notice how you feel in your surroundings. These feelings will lead you.

5. Watch for "clues" given to you by people, animals, books, media or other things in your experience.

6. Notice how smooth the experience feels. If it feels like a roller coaster ride, reevaluate and choose accordingly.

Day Nine
Our Great Mother Earth

I awoke early, feeling refreshed and ready for the day ahead. Thinking I would probably travel the highway from Tucson to Phoenix, I sat in stillness and connected to All That Is. The map would not be used once again, as I got the message to go north on what seemed to be a much less traveled road.

The route was a welcome change to the pace I had been keeping and I took advantage of the opportunity to just relax and take in the view. Thoughts were drifting through like mist through an early morning meadow. Where was I going? I had no idea, except north into the mountains. Hills and valleys, replete with shrubs, cacti, and trees, filled the field of view as I drove silently forward on my journey. I knew that wherever I was going, I would be rewarded richly with wonders yet unseen. Such had become this adventure.

I approached a fork in the road and would have gone toward Phoenix, but felt that was not the best choice. I am glad I listened to my inner feelings. A few miles beyond the fork in the road, I noticed a sign for Biosphere 2, Columbia University. I vaguely remembered an experiment in the early 1990's where eight people were sealed in a self-contained environment and stayed for up to two years. They grew all the food they ate and recycled all the air, water, and waste products. I had been given yet one more gift upon my journey.

Nestled in Canyon del Oro among the majesty of the Santa Catalina Mountains, Biosphere 2 gleams like a diamond on a velvet bed of green, sparkling with the brilliance of the desert sun. An area the size of three football fields contains structures, which paint a picture of white domes, arches and pyramids, interlaced with endless panes of glass, reflecting the gray and white clouds and blue sky above. It is a truly magnificent sight.

Biosphere 2

It was an educational campus, owned privately and under the leadership of Columbia University. Scientists and students were studying how our planet's ecosystems respond to an atmosphere of rising Carbon Dioxide levels, and other things affecting our Earth today. The structure contains a world of environments: Rainforest, Savanna, Desert, Marsh, Ocean, Farm, and Human Habitat. The Rainforest itself is five stories high and dominates the skyline.

The only part of the structure the public was allowed into was the human habitat that the original crews lived in for so long. There were walkways surrounding the environments and it was possible to watch the students and scientists at work. I was also fascinated to see the newest addition to the campus, a working telescope for the Astrophysics department. Astronomy was once again in my immediate view.

The concept of Biosphere 2 is based on the theory that life on Earth is self-regulating. As I sat at the table in the Human Habitat and felt the presence of those who had lived there, I began to feel the passion with which they lived out that experiment. They wanted to know how our environment affects us, and how we affect our environment. If only all of us could be so consciously aware of how we treat this world we call home.

I began to notice the potential and responsibility we have as human stewards of this planet. We have enormous potential and we can use it for the wellness of the planet, or to its detriment. As we pollute and use up our natural resources, we have to ask ourselves some important questions. Who will replenish them? What effect will our use of these things have on our planet and on us? These are the things being studied in this wonderful place.

What about the part we play in all of this? Are we willing to let things be done as they are at present? What can we do about it? These are questions we need to look at closely and make informed choices, based on both information and wisdom. Are we willing to look the other way when we see our environment destroyed? I knew I could no longer sit idly by and not speak out. Each voice makes a difference. Each person who adds the energy of hope and love makes an impact on the whole. We must make that stand if we intend to continue to interact and thrive upon this planet.

Having sat amidst the energy of this experiment, I was humbled within my world. I thought about the ultimate potential of creation we hold as human beings, and began to look at how we use it. I remember a statement in Walt Disney's Aladdin, when the Genie says he has "Phenomenal cosmic power, itty bitty living space". We have tremendous power of creation, enormous potential, and it is housed in this tiny living space called us, the human form. Or, to be more succinct, we are housed in it.

We are more than physical and our energy field extends far beyond the actual body. Energy is boundless and makes up everything in the universe. All energy is connected and so we are connected to all things and each other. Energy attracts like energy. When we give out love we attract love. As we put out thoughts, we attract like thoughts, through other people who "show up" in our lives. I'm sure we have all noticed some of these things happening as we live out our chosen roles.

This is how we create. We choose what it is we prefer and we "put it out to the universe". Consider it a silent prayer, thought in action. As a belief (which is pure energy) goes out, it attracts like beliefs to it. This is what is meant when I say what you give out you get back. We can do this consciously or unconsciously. When we begin to do this purposefully, consciously, the potential for miracles abounds. One person sending love creates a ripple effect and love will spread, slowly, but it will spread. Two or more, gathered for the same purpose, create love on an astronomical level. Our potential is HUGE.

Fear works the same way, as it too is energy. When we watch the news, for example, and see the fear portrayed, we can choose to add our fear to that, or we can choose to change the story, to add light and love to what we see and change the picture. Make no mistake; the choice is ours. It is always, all ways, our responsibility. Denying it or burying our heads in the sand will not change this fact. Blaming others or feeling there is nothing we can do will only keep us where we are.

I thought about how I want to use this energy and realized it was time to make changes in my life. I could no longer stay bogged down where I was. It was time to choose to move on and face the unknown, just as I was doing on this adventure. It is all too easy to stay in a cycle of discomfort, just because it is familiar. I could no longer live my life in the same old way.

I drove in silence, lost in thought, as the canvas outside the windows changed from one Masterpiece to another. The mountains held me within their grasp as the elevation increased. The temperature dropped to seventy-two degrees, a cool respite from the desert heat. Deep ravines and steep cliffs replaced the lower hills and valleys. Vegetation once more changed from desert plants to greener, denser trees.

There were large areas stripped of vegetation where ore was being mined. It felt as if Mother Earth had been sliced open and her insides exposed. Major surgery was taking place before my eyes. How could such beauty and peace of the last several miles be so quickly replaced with this feeling of sadness and desolation? It felt as if a violation had taken place and it added to my sadness.

I stopped at a Chamber of Commerce Tourist office in the mountains. It had an old, rusted mining cart out front filled with ores of every shape and color, free for the picking. I took a few colorful treasures, reminders of this adventure that I was only beginning to understand. I later realized my part in the whole picture. I felt sad for the depleting of minerals, crystals, and ores from Mother Earth, and yet I carried some of them home with me. I had much to learn. Without demand for such products, the destruction would not be taking place. I was as guilty as anyone else.

I was fighting loneliness again that day and realized I felt more alone in the towns with people than I did in the desert by myself. Alone, I felt peaceful and connected to a greater whole. Then I began to understand. Being physical beings, we will always crave the companionship of others, but that is not all we are. Sometimes we have to be by ourselves to realize we are ONE.

It is truly not the destination that is important, but the journey that takes us there. We are being divinely guided every step of the way. The more we listen to and follow our feelings, the smoother the journey will be. I was hearing The Guys less and less as I progressed on this adventure and was wondering if I was missing something. I was beginning to understand that when I heard nothing, I was in the right place. It was when I did not listen they needed to shout.

I continued north until I came to Globe, connecting with another road leading to Phoenix. I knew it was time to go in that direction; I had seen what I was led to see that day. I arrived in Phoenix at rush hour and found a motel as quickly as I could. I was tired and there were so many emotions running through my being I felt swamped. I talked to my husband and although I missed him, I did not want to return. I knew I was holding onto the past and didn't know how to let go. I wanted what once was and knew it could never be again.

In the motel office was a man dressed in shabby clothing, rocking a vending machine and I took a wide berth around him. As I returned to my room I wondered why I was afraid of him. Was I afraid because of his appearance and actions, or had I been in danger? I did not want to judge anyone because of appearance, but wondered if that is what I had just done. I asked God to show me the difference between fear that warns us of danger, and fear from learned beliefs such as prejudice of appearance, color, or creed. I knew I would be shown the answer when the time was right.

I had a throbbing headache, a toothache, and my nose was bleeding from the changes in altitude. I knew these were just signs of my discontent and fear and would leave when I worked through the fear I was facing. Who was I? What was I doing? What would happen when I got home? I chose to let the fear move through my being like a breeze through a screen. I drifted into a fitful sleep and dreamed of people doing something to my feet and of an acquaintance, Susan Stark, a gifted singer/songwriter.

Conversation with The Guys:

Pat: Why have I been drawn to open vortices and light columns in so many places?

Guys: It is time to bring more powerful concentrations of light to the area and you have the ability to do it. Thank you.

Pat: Then that is only one of the things I was brought here to do?

Guys: Yes, one of the many. Everything is going perfectly. Be kind to yourself and do not judge yourself otherwise. Be happy. Choose joy. And so it is.

Lesson from the day:
What we put out, we get back.

I rode through the mountains that were being stripped of their minerals and exposed to the elements that drained them of their essence. When I took some of those same minerals home, I realized that I helped create the problem I saw before me. What we give out, we truly get back.

My desire for these minerals, along with many others, created the miner's scramble to produce them. It is known as supply and demand. We blame the mining on greed of the people doing the mining, but in truth, if the demand was not there, they would no be doing so. We have to look at what we desire, what we "put out to the universe". It is the energy of that thought that creates what comes back to us. This goes for everything in life, not just today's example of mining.

How do you change what you put out?

1. First and foremost – Know, without a shadow of a doubt, that you are creating what you see.

2. Be honest. Take responsibility for your choices. Do NOT blame the ones who give you what you wanted. You asked for it.

3. Think about the consequences of your choices. Who and what will be affected by those choices? In this case it was Mother Earth.

4. Make choices that will give you what you desire, without **harming** another person, place or thing. This does not mean others may not feel "hurt" by your choices, but you will cause no "harm". Hurt is something a person *feels*, determined by beliefs and memories of past actions. Harm is physical or emotional damage.

5. What you give out, you WILL get back. It is sometimes called Karma. It is physics, not philosophy. You may get it directly back or it may come back in another time and place.

6. Always, all ways, use this as your guide to what energy you give out.

Day Ten
Answered Prayer

I woke in the morning with a song running over and over in my head. It is called "Lord, Don't Move the Mountain", a song written by Doris Akers and sung by Susan. It is about enduring and overcoming trials. It tells God not to move the mountain, but give me the strength to climb it, to learn from the experience and grow stronger in the process. I had the song on a tape she recorded called "Canción de la Loba/Song of the She Wolf" and knew I would be listening to it often that day.

As I walked to the office to turn in my key, I saw a man on a stepladder painting the outside of the building. He smiled at me and said "Good morning". He was a very pleasant man and I saw that he worked for the motel. I also realized he was the man I saw shaking the vending machine the night before. He may have been trying to fix a problem with the machine when I saw him shake it, I never did find out, but I did realize I had allowed my fear to make judgments that kept me away. Half of my prayer was answered. I knew what it was like to be in fear because of learned beliefs.

Emotions were near the surface as I left Phoenix early that morning. I was also experiencing a lot of pain in my feet and it was difficult to walk. I suspected it had something to do with the dream, but didn't know what. I popped Susan's tape into the player and listened to the song I had dreamed about. And I cried. I felt weird, like my body was being torn apart and readjusted at all levels. There is no other way I could describe it. I felt like my molecules had been scrambled and were being rearranged.

A while later I came to a rest area and, still feeling a bit drained from the experience, I pulled into it for a break. I was going to get out of the car and take a walk to clear and center myself. There was a van parked in the parking lot and a crew of men in orange jumpsuits. I realized they were prisoners who were doing roadwork and were taking a break with their guards.

They watched me closely as I parked the car and I had a prickly feeling of fear, as if something was not quite right. The rest of my prayer was being answered. I was being shown what it means to have fear that warns us of danger. There was no judgment of these men, as either good or bad, but there was a sense of foreboding. I chose to leave the rest stop and continue on my journey, thanking God for such a meaningful answer to my prayer.

I was beginning to see the wonder of the Universe and how it works. What we ask for is given. I thought of all the adages, such as "God works in mysterious ways, His wonders to perform". I wondered how often I have had prayers answered and had not noticed. Had I been too busy to see that all prayers are answered? It is all too easy to discard events as coincidence. I knew I would no longer choose to be unconscious and unseeing, and I asked God to remind me if I became remiss. Maybe I was learning after all.

As I drove, the scene sped by in a methodical cadence. Saguaro cacti were replaced with more clumpy bushes. A town I drove through announced the local eating establishment, *Willow's Restaurant*. My friends called me Willow at the time and I felt welcome, at home. Straight roads curled into serpentine switchbacks as the elevation increased, once again heralding an evergreen forest.

I was approaching Prescott and the view was spectacular. Some of the switchbacks were so dramatic they turned one hundred and seventy degrees, heading back almost parallel to the road I had just traveled. Twenty miles an hour was the average speed limit and even that left little time to admire the scenery. I stopped and stood under a tree, gazing at the beauty before me, and prayed.

Switchbacks to Prescott

I prayed for God to send me someone in this wonderful land, who would teach me, to show me what I had come here to find. I sensed the stillness and a knowing slowly dawned upon me. The answer came. "Take heart. Soon." I would know soon. I felt like the trees were embracing me. I had once more become a part of the world around me.

If you want to see the country, travel the back roads. It may take longer, but the journey far outweighs the time spent getting to the goal. This was once again proving my belief that it is the journey that is important, not the destination. I thought of all the things I would have missed, had I not taken this particular route, this particular journey, and I was grateful for my life, for the privilege of experiencing such a wonderful world, in such a marvelous way. I felt truly blessed.

I felt like my energy was drained from the earlier experiences of the day. I was in need of recharging and had come to the exact right place. It was too early to check into the motel, so I donned my hiking gear and headed into the forest. Old growth forests contain a level of energy that is found in very few places on our planet. Trees, like all other things on our planet, hold energy and old trees hold the world within their branches.

Huge evergreen trees grew to what seemed like infinity. Branches and treetops met sky in a never-ending kiss, exchanging moisture and oxygen. Boulders emerged from the ground like relics of an ancient past, rising from the ground in solid triumph. Peace was felt throughout this place, along with strength and a sense of belonging. Fear, doubt and all human emotions were an unknown illusion to these ancient ones.

New life budded and sprang from the ground, surrounded and safe in this world. Birds sat in silence, watching this intruder to their world, occasionally flying down for a closer look. They were curious. The watcher became the watched as this dance began. Their world became my own, shared, experienced, loved. Their energy became my own as I breathed in the world around me, once again feeling my wholeness.

I walked, first the paths that led up the mountains, and then the areas yet unexplored. I sat on rocks, hugged trees, talked to the wildlife, talked to God, and shared life with the world around me. I was learning that to share life with this world, with Mother Earth, we must involve ourselves in the process. Just as life, we cannot share if we sit and watch. We must become a part of what we are watching. We then become the experience.

At one point I felt a connection so strong, it was as if a thousand pound weight were pulling me to the ground, enveloping me it its midst. I could feel the "weight of the world" as

I felt its presence. It was a rather disconcerting feeling. I was one with the Earth.

As I walked back down the mountain, I noticed a stand of trees to my left. It was a circular grouping and there were two ponderosa pines directly in front of me, forming a gate, an entry into this circle, as if in invitation. As I entered between these two trees, I felt a surge of energy surround me. I entered from the East and went directly to the northernmost tree, putting my forehead to the trunk and clearing my mind, opening to the energy within. This was repeated to the West and South.

I then stood in silence at the center of this circle, listening to the world within and the world without. It was a sacred experience, difficult to share because it cannot be reproduced in mere words. As I left through the gateway, a portal between those stately pines, I noticed the energy had increased to astronomical proportions. It was electric. As I turned and looked back, I sensed a vortex of energy that had opened up within that circle, connecting Heaven and Earth. It was an awesome event, a sacred rite, shared with the Universe itself.

Returning to the car, I realized what we miss when we do not take the time to share ourselves with our environment. It is here for us always, all ways, and we seldom take or make the time to share such moments. We need to do more of these things. As we learn to open to the world around us, to feel the love that is inherent in the Universe and all who inhabit it, we will learn to value ourselves as part of that whole and to love all we share it with.

Entering the town of Prescott is like stepping into another time. The streets are lined with old buildings, including an old bar with the traditional swinging saloon doors. It is a refreshing step into a slower pace, a quieter time. There is much to be said for going slower, living at a less stressful pace. Disease is largely a result of stress, for stress creates blocks in the energy within the body and blocks create the environment for disease. Perhaps we need to take a step backward, to a healthier pace for us, and our world.

I was feeling better and took advantage of the slower pace. I got some films developed and treated myself to a delight of wine, cheese and crackers. It was a delicious change of pace and a marvelous opportunity to unwind. Sleep would be pleasant that night, drifting into clouds of soft dreams and pleasant memories.

Conversation with The Guys:

Pat: Was I correct in my understanding of learned fear and actual fear of danger?

Guys: Yes. They feel quite different, do they not?

Pat: Yes. True fear of danger seems to make my skin crawl. It's very creepy, for lack of a better term.

Guys: We see that often. It is important to know the difference. Learned fear is someone's idea of what to be afraid of and it is important to see it for what it is. Separation. Prejudice. There are many forms with many names. All are means to keep you in separation and they are the cause of all conflict.

Lesson from the day: Fear & Prejudice

What is fear and why do we have it? There are many reasons and one of the biggest is the belief that we are separate from everyone else. As long as we believe we are separate, we believe that one is better or less than, right or wrong, black or white, etc. We believe others have power over us and we feel a need to defend ourselves. One leads to another in a never-ending loop.

Originally, fear was used as a survival tool. This is the fear of harm, like I felt with the prisoners. Hunters used it to warn them of danger so they could live for another hunt. As we developed other means of survival and life became safer, we forgot it was a tool of safety and turned it outward to others. The fear manifested as prejudice. We saw everything outside ourselves as a threat.

We looked at groups of individuals with similar qualities that were different than our own and feared they would harm us, like I feared the man shaking the vending machine. We feared there was not enough so we had to take all there was for ourselves and let the others go without. This caused the others to fight for some of what we had. Anyone being of different color, size, or difference in any way became the enemy.

What do we do with this? How do we take this knowledge and turn it back to a feeling of unity and peace? Follow these few steps and see what a joy life will truly become.

1. When you feel fear, notice what it is.

2. Are you afraid for your safety?

3. Are you judging the situation by what you have been taught?

4. Ask yourself if you have ever done what the person you fear is doing. Remember why you did it.

5. If you are in judgment, be it color, religion, politics, etc., put it aside and see what you see without the former teachings.

6. Remember the only thing that makes you different from the person you fear is your experience. You had different teachers, parents, social activities, religions, etc. Inside, you are the same.

Day Eleven
Day of Rest

As I sat in stillness that morning, I was told that I needed to rest for the day. I had hit the ground running ten days earlier and had not stopped since. I decided it would be a day to be a human being, not a human doing.

I treated myself to a restaurant breakfast and as I sat, I sensed a conscious energy in the seat across from me. This consciousness seemed to say, "You are almost ready. Soon." and then it disappeared as quickly as it appeared. Had it not been for the marvelous connection I had been experiencing with God and the Universe, I would have found this to be strange, but it was becoming amazingly natural.

The pool was a refreshing change from the one in Tucson. The water was surprisingly cold, due to the cold nights in the mountains. The difference in altitude was about a mile. I decided to swim a few laps and was rewarded with a heartbeat matching the cadence of a machine gun. I was, at first, upset because I thought I was in better shape; and then I remembered the altitude. What a difference a mile makes!

When I was preparing to make the journey, I had felt drawn to many names and places, but there were two that had been screamed in my ear, into my awareness. The first was Alamagordo, which was to become permanently ingrained in my heart, and the second was Prescott. As I was to discover my deep connection to the first, I was to do the same with the second.

I had never been one to take time for myself, to make time for the saner things in life. It felt like to slow down was actually going backwards. The slower pace was something I had not experienced without chagrin. Just lying in the sun at the pool was a challenge. I had that old pull to get up and DO something. I felt like I was wasting time. My mind kept re-minding me of all the things I could or should be doing. A dragonfly landed on my leg and stayed there for some time, staring at me as I stared at it. It seemed to say it's OK to just BE.

I realized what we, as humans, do. We get ourselves going faster and faster, building up momentum to keep us moving, in perpetual motion. We do this because, if we stop, we have to face ourselves. It is easier to live with the distractions we create. I looked at my life and began to see all the ways I had done this. Work, hobbies, projects, and television were just some of the things I had chosen in my life to keep me busy, away from myself. I would no longer find this to be acceptable.

Facing ourselves is a wonderful experience. When the old emotions that arise are faced, we can choose to keep them or let them move through, changing us forever. DNA is actually transformed and changed in the process. We are not stuck in the old habits unless we choose to stay there. This would no longer be an excuse. If I stayed the same, I knew it was my choice. It was time to take full responsibility for my actions.

Taking responsibility means never blaming anyone else for anything we are being, doing, having or feeling. It means not blaming ourselves for anything we've said or done. We did the best we could, given the person we were at the time. We may choose to do it differently now, but that is because we learned from our past experience. Taking responsibility means choosing what we most desire to do in life and acting on it. And it means being aware of the myriad of choices that are available to us at all times. Responsibility is NOT blame.

I knew that by taking responsibility for my actions, old and new, I was not taking blame. Blame is a judgment of right or wrong, based on learned beliefs. I would not choose to take blame for my actions, but I would own the responsibility for my choices. The difference is astronomical. Blame keeps us in a belief that we are good or bad, that we are victims or perpetrators. It keeps us in a self-sustained loop, repeating the same old choices, over and over.

The truth is we do the best we can in each moment, in each thing we experience. This is a fact we need to understand and to accept. It will change our world. When we give up blame, we allow for the natural state of love to flow freely through our being. We are love in its truest form.

I decided to go back to the forest in the afternoon and looked for my watch so I would know the time. It was nowhere to be found, which was strange, as I had few belongings to look through. I got the message that I needed to let go of time and when I had done that I would find the watch.

I brought a large towel with me. Finding the circular group of trees from the previous day, I put it on the ground and laid on my back, face to the sun, surrounded by this sentry of trees. I began to feel the old feelings of wasting time and realized that true "wasting" of time is to use the time to keep us from ourselves. Spending time with oneself can never be a waste of time or anything else.

It is easy to deplete our energy by keeping ourselves too busy to tend to our own health and well being. I had started to do this by keeping the pace at which I had begun this adventure. It was time to replenish that energy, to create well being once again. Health is our natural state of being, and will stay that way until we interfere with the process.

There were places in this forest that felt so high in energy my skin actually felt as if it were buzzing. I hiked the mountain, sharing and taking in the energy around me. Trees and ground, rocks and sky became one more interactive canvas, exchanging energy in yet one more dance of creation and sharing. Once again I felt energized and whole.

The park in town is a lovely mural, painted in the bright greens of grass and trees. Dotting this scene are paths of brown and white. Park benches filled with people eating, reading and taking in the beauty line the paths. Dogs on leashes bounce along on feet of springs and children glide by on bicycles, not a care in the world. Birds herald the coming of anything new, surveying the scene they inhabit.

I took the time to sit on the grass, my back to the trunk of an ancient, majestic tree and breathed in the scene surrounding me. I felt joy, peace and serenity. Seldom had I taken the time to experience such simple pleasure, such joy at nature's wonders. Nature is not a thing that we see around us, but a friend we share our very existence with.

I drifted back to the motel that evening, as if in a dream. I was renewed in body and spirit, ready for the day ahead. As I packed my few belongings for the coming day, I found my watch on top of my suitcase, in plain sight, right where I had looked earlier. I did not question why I missed it before. It was not there – and then it was. I was learning that all things are possible; we need only believe and trust in that higher power. God does truly work in strange ways, His wonders to perform.

Conversation with The Guys:

Pat: Wow, what a rejuvenating day it has been. You were right. Taking today off to recharge my batteries was heavenly. I loved spending time in the forest with the trees. The energy there is awesome.

Guys: Know this; it is almost the time when you will need to do many things in ways that are not familiar to you. You needed this time to kick back and regroup your forces. You were becoming depleted. It will be necessary, now more than ever, for you to take care of your energy requirements. Do not do more than your body can handle. Be kind to yourself and take care of that body; it gets tired if you push it too hard. You need to keep yourself at optimum levels of energy. You will know more soon.

Do not fear you have come all this way for nothing. That is as far from the truth as it gets. You will be seeing soon why you have come. Many things are happening in preparation for where you are going. There will soon be a time when all of this makes sense, some on this trip, some after you return home.

*As you enjoyed the trees, they also enjoyed you. It is not often they get someone in their presence that **consciously** knows you are one. As they gave to you, you gave to them.*

Take care now and take heart, for all is perfect in God's Kingdom and you are learning much. Have no vision of what this will look like. Be open to all. Know that all things, even if they seem like nothing, are never that. Keep your ears and eyes open. Your destiny lies at your fingertips. Soon Dear One, soon.

Lesson from the day: BEing is as important as DOing

We spend our lives keeping so busy we have no time to get to know ourselves. We use our jobs, hobbies, and other distractions to keep us from having to feel what we fear we will feel if we meet ourselves face to face. We keep "doing" things until we become overcome with fatigue or immersed in stress.

We need to take the time, make the time, to spend with ourselves in peace and quiet. This is where we will find our hearts. It is in our hearts that we will find there is no need to do anything. There is just a feeling of peace at our core. This is where we can just be who we are. While there, there is nothing to prove, do or become. You simply are. This is beingness at its best.

To get to that place of being, try these few simple ideas.

1. Make time to be alone for a while.

2. Ignore the thoughts that tell you to DO the laundry, GO shopping, or any other action.

3. Feel the joy of the moment.

4. BE one with your environment.

5. Make an agreement with yourself to do this at least once a day. It will refresh you in body, mind and spirit.

Day Twelve
Facing Mortality

Slept fitfully at best and woke up suddenly in the morning feeling stark terror throughout my being. I had been dreaming about having abdominal surgery and was told I had very little chance of survival. Some dreams are forgotten soon after waking and some stay with us much longer. This one felt so real that the feeling of terror would not leave. I felt like I was going to die.

I realized this must be what it's like to get a diagnosis of cancer or some other fatal condition and be told you have little time to live. It was terrifying. My mind battled with my heart. I knew what I had to do; I had to face, accept, and overcome the fear of death.

I asked why I was given this dream. Spiritually, I knew I could not die, for we are eternal, always and forevermore. We are. We exist. This is a law of the Universe that will never change. Energy can neither be created nor destroyed, but it does change form. Bodies will cease to exist, but the energy within will remain in another form. Our spirit will live.

Bodies on the other hand hold ingrained beliefs within the DNA. These are inbred for survival and when we feel threatened, the body goes into fear posture. It is as if the body is a separate entity with a mind of its own. In fact, that is not a bad analogy. A large percentage of our DNA is called "Junk DNA", mostly because science does not know what it does. I believe it holds emotional beliefs, much like the databanks in our computers hold information. Beliefs are pure energy and are acquired from eons of experience. Thought is also pure energy; my body thought it was going to die and I felt terror. Fear In the Body is a FIB. We have to expose the lie.

As a nurse I had seen many people who approached their illnesses with apparently no fear of death. Even those with terminal conditions, facing death and saying they were prepared, fought for their lives when it was time to transition to another plane of existence. For years I wondered why. Why do we fight so hard to stay alive? Is it a fear of the unknown before us? Even spiritual teachers who believed in an afterlife would fight to stay alive. Was it something ingrained in our physical bodies, in our DNA, that fought to survive?

Tears silently slid down my face, my body quivering with fear. Knowing this was just triggered from a dream did not lessen the intensity of the experience. It was real. I knew I had to let go of who I was. I had to let the old me die, so I consciously left my old self in the mountains of Arizona. I also made a choice to keep the wisdom and love that was part of the old me and integrate it into who I was becoming. I found myself wishing I knew who that was.

I drove through the mountains, letting go of the old "baggage," the things about myself I no longer felt represented who I wanted to be. I knew I was saying goodbye to what was no longer. I also knew I was writing the script of who and what I would become. I needed to listen to my heart, hear my heart, and create what I found there. This was my script, my life, and I had to create it based on what I knew was right for me, not what I thought someone else wanted me to be, or some other outside influence.

Too often we create our lives around what others believe is right for us. We are influenced by parents, teachers, clergy, friends, and even the media. Our society bombards us with its perception of perfection twenty four hours a day. We are taught to conform to the beliefs of others and we are taught to feel guilty when we choose opposing beliefs. We must listen to our hearts wherein all the wisdom lies. Only there will we find what is right for us.

I needed to find the courage to follow my heart, even though it would not be seen as acceptable to some of my friends and family. I no longer fit the mold that I had so painstakingly created for myself so many years ago. My beliefs had changed. My likes and dislikes were no longer the same, even my physical body was changing dramatically. I was no longer stiff and inflexible as I had been. I could, quite literally, no longer maintain the same old posture.

Such was my state of mind when I arrived in Jerome, a fascinating town, built on a mountainside. The buildings sit on the edge of the slopes as if it took all their energy to maintain their tenuous balance. It was begun as a copper mining town, named for Winston Churchill's grandfather, New York financier, Eugene Jerome. Today it is lined with quaint little shops, filled with wonderful objects of art. The view was awesome and I took some time to walk around and see the world as an eagle would view it, from this precarious perch.

It was a wonderful distraction and kept me from facing the fear that my body was feeling. As soon as I was back on the road however, the feeling once again became too strong to avoid. The closer I got to Sedona, the stronger it got. It seemed like the fear would just keep building and building until it was unbearable. I decided that this fear of death, because of its intensity, must be eons old. Perhaps it is a primal belief, instilled in our DNA when we first began to believe we are separate from our source.

I had been looking forward to seeing Sedona, as it has been talked of so often as one of the high-energy spots on the planet. I found this to be true. I also found that whatever degree of emotional issues we are feeling when we go there will be magnified proportionately. I felt like my body was coming apart. It was dying. I felt awful.

I stopped at a Forest Service office to get a map and a pass to park at the major vortexes in the area, and was amazed at how commercial the town was. I had expected a quiet place and was surprised to see jeep tours and all the other commercial things you would see in any tourist area. I had gone with expectations and they were not what I found. I realize that when this happens it is not a problem with the place, but with the expectation.

Hiking the major vortex areas was unique. Had I done this at any other time, it would have been a pleasantly enlightening experience. Doing it at the height of this emotional/physical crisis was extremely challenging. I wanted to run away from there. It was too painful to feel this intensity of emotion, and at the same time I knew I needed to be there. I had chosen, on some level, to work through the fear in that way at that time.

Looking back at it, I believe I chose to do it that way to move through things that would normally have taken weeks, if not months to move through. I chose to do it "head on", in a manner I could not ignore. It is not something I would recommend for anyone else or for myself again for that matter. It was one of the most challenging things I have ever done. In hindsight however, I am glad I did it that way. It enabled me to move forward much more quickly.

The rest of the afternoon was spent visiting the vortex areas. All were beautiful, and the most meaningful for me was Boynton Canyon. As I hiked the hillsides I was able to feel a calming effect of the chaotic energies I was working through. I also found it interesting when I was told this area has the highest incidence of UFO sightings in the country. It seems space was to become a theme of this adventure.

Sedona

The motels in the area are in the pricier category, again conforming to the tourist status. I sometimes find it challenging to understand why the most natural things seem to be the most exploited. I understand the theory of supply and demand, but there is a part of me that finds it hard to chew, gritty in my teeth. It is hard for me to put a price on God's wonders of creation, but that is me. Sometimes I see things from a different perspective than most.

My husband called that night and I began to cry. I had trouble talking. He asked me to come home and I could not. I wanted to go home and didn't know where home was. I wanted to go and I wanted to stay. As painful as it was, I knew I had to be there. I felt like a thousand years of emotional debris was being released from my DNA. When I hung up the phone, I began to sob huge hysterical sobs. I cried until I could cry no more, all the tears being released from my body like a cleansing waterfall. It was a catharsis.

I was confused and exhausted. Nothing made sense. I knew something huge was happening within my being, but I had no idea what it was. I also knew I needed to let this move through. I prayed for clarity, for answers, and fell into an exhausted sleep, hoping answers would come while I slept.

Conversation with The Guys:

Pat: OK, would you like to tell me what the heck is going on? I woke up last night with a dream that I would probably die in a surgery I was being prepared for. I had similar dreams all night and my body feels like it is dying.

Guys: You are dying, dying to the old so you can support the new. It is important – PARAMOUNT – that you allow for this to move through. We cannot stress this enough. LET THIS MOVE THROUGH.

Your body is being cleared of old beliefs. Some of these go back eons and are inherent in the human form, in the physical being. All of you will have to do this before you will be able to hold the higher vibrations to evolve. You are being helped to lead the way. There is no mistake you are where you are on this day. The energy here is helping you to move through this. We understand that this feels terrible to you, but do not let that deter you from your task at hand.

You also said you would like to go home. You can do this if you wish.

Pat: No. I only want to do that so I won't feel this pain I am in. I went through something similar when I worked through the ego a few years ago, but this is different.

Guys: Yes, it is. This is clearing the way for a quantum leap, if you will. This is similar to what your man called Jesus did in the desert. He had to be there to do this same thing. It was necessary for him to do this before he could do what he did later.

Pat: I was hoping to meet someone here that could help me with all of this. I prayed for such a thing and it seems I must do this on my own. I know if a prayer seems not to be answered, it is only my perception of it that is not correct. All prayers are answered, just not in the way we prefer. I was thinking of a physical being and it is you who are helping.

Guys: This is so My Dear One, AND this prayer will also be answered. It will be answered in its own perfect timing. It may be on this present trip, and it may be at a later time, that you are not to know. Right now there is only ONE thing that is of absolute necessity. Rest and let this move through. You have worked hard today and MUCH has been done. Allow for this to precipitate out of the body. Tomorrow will be a different day than today.

Know you are loved and that you are doing much, not only for yourself, but for mankind. That will become evident to you at a later time. Sleep well My Child, sleep well. We will see you in your sleep.

Lesson from the day: Letting go.

We become accustomed to feeling what we know. Even if it does not feel good, we tend to stay with it because it is familiar. There are times in our lives when we are faced with the choice of letting go of the old structures and beliefs to make room for new, healthier ones.

This was my lesson on that day and it changed my life in ways I cannot begin to tell you. Some were subtle and some dramatic, and all were crucial to becoming what I am now. It was very tempting to go home and stop the process, but I knew it had to be done.

When you are facing situations and feelings that are challenging at best, remember these few steps and march forward with hope and love in your hearts.

1. Identify the feeling you are experiencing.

2. Refuse to back away from the process.

3. Allow yourself to let the energy of the feelings move through like wind through a screen.

4. Acknowledge the feelings kicked up by the one moving through. Cry if you need to. Honor what you need to keep the process moving.

5. Rest when you are done. Give yourself time to recharge and get to know yourself.

6. Love the new you.

Day Thirteen
Turning Point

I woke the next morning feeling drained, but better. I had intended to go north, but was once again guided in a different direction. I found myself headed south, retracing my path of the day before. After driving for a while, I found myself heading east on a well-traveled road, and eventually coming to a sign which said, "Montezuma Castle National Monument".

Montezuma Castle

I was in the Verde Valley, once home to the Sinagua and Hohokam (Pima) tribes. The Pima were skillful farmers who watered by irrigation and lived in one-room houses made of poles, sticks, and mud, built on terraces overlooking their fields in the bottomlands. The Sinagua were fine artisans and made stone tools, such as knives, axes, hammers and manos and metates for grinding corn.

They later began building pueblos on hilltops or in the cliffs. Today there remains a five story, twenty room cliff dwelling, that is quite well preserved. Walkways meander through the area and the view of the dwelling is spectacular. It was a wonderful, respite from the emotional stress of the day before. I felt renewed and ready to continue my journey.

As I was leaving the area I passed a small booth filled with Native American crafts, set up on a gravel parking area. In this booth was a wonderful Native American couple. He was of Apache descent and she a Navajo and they were selling their wares. The man was one of the most wonderfully funny people I have met. They were selling, among other things, minia-ture replicas of burden baskets and he told me why they have bells attached to them. It seems that mothers-in-law were not allowed to speak with their sons-in-law, so bells were attached to the baskets. The bells were a warning that the other was approaching and must leave. He laughed as he told me this and other stories about his people.

The woman with him had no such sense of humor. The more he told stories and laughed, the more serious she became. He seemed to enjoy this interplay and told more and more stories. She made some fry bread for me and when I put both honey and sugar on it, he started to tease me and said, "I never said you were a piggy." It was as if I had known him for centuries as we laughed together. I bought a craft item to give to a friend and made a comment that it was so nice I thought I might keep it myself. He called me an Indian-Giver. His humor was infectious and we bantered that one for a few minutes as we both roared with laughter. I left with a feeling of love in my heart.

I have often found that we are afraid to speak to people about anything we think will make them uncomfortable. Because we judge these things in advance, we miss opportunities to meet people from their hearts. We don't give them a chance to show us who they really are and we miss the chance to share in such wonderful interactions. We have all been taught many stereotypes and I was seeing how injurious these are. This man taught me to have no expectations or judgments of who or what people should be. Without expectations and fear I was able to see him as exactly who he was, and I found that to be perfect.

We are taught to be careful, to be politically correct, to not "rock the boat", and we are taught to fear those we do not know, or who look different than ourselves. I am not saying I think it is a good idea to act foolishly, to go up to total strangers on the street IF we feel there is danger. We need to use the intuitive sense we were born with. I am saying that I think we have swung too far to the side of fear and cut ourselves off from the world around us. I knew I would not do so again.

I found myself on the highway north, heading toward Flagstaff, which is where I had wanted to go in the morning. As I approached an exit for Sedona, I found myself turning onto it. I was, once again, returning to Sedona, yet from a different direction. It seems there was something I had not yet accomplished there.

Approaching Sedona from the east was a scenic thrill. Red rocks filled the scene from one side to the other. It was as if an artist spilled cans of desert red paint over the entire canvas. Green trees and shrubs dotted the landscape, stippled with a stiff brush. The sky shone brightly above, blue and white, in relief. God spread his hands and molded visions of red clay into solid, earthly form.

I stopped to walk a path to Bell Rock, a spectacular formation at the location of one of the vortexes. The experience
was exhilarating, yet there was a feeling of things not being
complete. This was not what I came back here to do. I was
not sure what I was missing, but this was not it. I needed to
move on.

As I approached the center of town, I found myself facing
a gray, two-story building with a sign that said "Psychic
Readings". It was too early and was not yet open, but two of
the women who worked there were waiting on the porch for
the owner to unlock the door. We talked for a few minutes
and pleasantly passed the time. It was a lovely place, offering
many things, such as several varieties of crystals and other
handcrafted items.

I do not usually put a lot of stock in readings; they show
us probabilities, not certainties, but I felt the need to do so that
day. It was the turning point of my journey. I had been hearing
God, The Guys, for some time, yet there were times I felt the
connection was not pure, or I questioned my own ability to
hear clearly. The woman who did the Psychic Readings also
taught classes in channeling. I decided to stay and meet her.

I knew the potential we all hold for this connection, yet
was unclear about how to connect wherever and whenever I
wished. I was hearing The Guys quite well by now, but sometimes felt like I was being interfered with. At times I felt
confused about what I was hearing and what to believe.

I told her nothing of this or anything about myself. As
we began to talk, she sensed what I needed. She told me I was
channeling, picking up energies that are not of the highest
quality and getting dis-information along with higher information. Her guides gave me a warning that I am not in control
of my channeling and I can be. Her guides were so insistent on
helping me with this that she asked if I would be willing for

her to close her store and compress her channeling class for me. I was thrilled.

She taught me a technique that enabled me to connect with God, The Guys, in a simple and direct way, whenever I choose. It was the turning point in my life, one of those serendipitous moments in time when everything that was ceases to be and the world opens before you with new meaning and grace.

She asked if I would like to know my life purpose and I said yes. She "read my energy field" and said that my Spiritual Purpose is to initiate a change in the consciousness for others through inner plane development. I am to help others heal diffusion of soul by raising the energy of humanity and moving to another level. She saw that I would be channeling, writing and lecturing in my "future".

She also warned me that I tend to start out strong and give up before I reach my goal. I was told to keep that in my awareness so I could overcome it. I was told to take supplements so I don't burn out. Selenium, B6 and other important things were to be added when I channel. I was also told to eat chocolate before I channel and I needed no prompting for that! I would not be able to work with the public until I created a pure environment to channel pure energy.

It seemed like months of learning took place in about an hour and a half. I was reeling from the information and felt a bit like "road kill". In spite of all that, I left there feeling exhilarated, knowing I had met the sage I was seeking and praying to meet. The experience was so profound that it left me in a state of exhaustion. I was drained yet at the same time, strangely energized.

I had been asking God to send me someone to show me the way, to help me to see my path, and I had been led to this place. There are no mistakes in this Universe. What we ask for is given. Even though I left Sedona earlier, I was led back to this teacher, and I was given the lesson I so needed. My prayer had been answered in a way I could not have begun to imagine.

I left Sedona before sunset and drove through some of the most spectacular scenery to date, arriving in Flagstaff about seven p.m. I knew I had just had the experience of a lifetime. I was not allowed to tape the conversation, so I spent the evening writing down the experience so I would remember as much of it as I could.

There was no conversation with The Guys that night because I was unable to do another thing. I finished the recollection of the day's events and fell into heavy sleep as soon as my head "hit the pillow."

Lesson from the day:
Prayers are always answered

We speak often of prayer, but what is it and how does it work? First of all we need to look at the difference between prayer and meditation. Prayer has often been seen as asking for something. It is a one-way communication. Meditation has been understood as communing with a higher consciousness or, in some cases, a means of relaxation. That is a two-way communication.

Either one of these is prayer. When you get to a place of knowing or "feeling" what you need, the energy goes out to the higher consciousness and it is received by that consciousness. It is from there that what you are broadcasting is heard and acted upon by that consciousness.

Answers can come to you in any way. When you have no preconceived ideas of what that has to look like, it can be recognized as the answer. The thing to do is recognize it when it's been answered. That is sometimes where everything gets caught up in human thinking. Expectations are dangerous to the truth because they keep you from seeing what is there in front of you.

These are just a few simple steps to consciously create the prayers you prefer.

1. Understand that the higher consciousness hears what is in your heart, not your head. Be VERY clear which one you are broadcasting. It hears what you feel, not what you say (unless they match).

2. Trust that the prayer will be answered.

3. Have no expectation about how the answer must manifest. If you are hungry, love chocolate and ask for nourishment, you may get scrambled eggs. The prayer has been answered.

4. Do not blame God or any other manifestation of All That Is for the prayer you did not recognize as answered.

5. If you did not see the answer, you missed it. Look again.

Day Fourteen
Valuing Life

I awoke to a chilly, damp and rainy morning. Had expected to go east and went north instead, heading toward the Grand Canyon. I questioned myself, started north and turned around a few times, then finally decided I was going in the best direction after all. Heavy clouds clung to the sky like weighted cotton balls, soaked in dark, inky water. Slowly these clouds began to lighten and blue sky began to peek between them.

The road stretched ahead, winding through forested mountains and I came upon a building on the side of the road. It was a small, elongated building, one end wider and taller than the other, and coming to a point on the roof of the higher side. The sides were short and made of stone, with the shingled roof extending almost to the ground. The narrow end had a wooden door, fastened with a strap, covering its width. The sign out front said, "Chapel of the Dove".

Stepping into the chapel was like stepping into a magical space. The floor was covered with coarse gravel. Benches filled the space, and the walls and ceiling were covered with written notes and prayers. The far end of the building was wider and taller than the entrance. The taller end was filled with windows, forming a large triangle or pyramid shape. Pine trees and mountains were viewed through this marvel.

The effect was awesome. There was a feeling of reverence in this place that defied its simple appearance. I decided to try the technique I was taught the day before and see what message I received. I received this message, which I wrote and left on the floor by the window. **"Know that you art one with the Universe, and as He is, so shall you be."**

I had been alone in this amazing place and as I was leaving I met a couple from Fort Worth, Texas, who arrived with their nine-year old grandson. They had brought him here when he was three months old and were now bringing him back to revisit this wonder. Such was the magic of this place.

Chapel of the Dove

As I continued, tall pines turned into less dense forest as the miles slid by. Deeper, denser shrubs replaced taller trees and changed the canvas to yet one more masterpiece. As I drove I felt like I was being tested in my faith of myself. I had been questioning myself about my direction throughout the day and knew I needed to get out of my own way and trust. I needed to stop judging every move I made.

I also realized I needed to value things in life that I never valued before. I had not taken the time to appreciate what was in front of me. I think we get so busy that we go through life without seeing it. Before I started this adventure, I would drive without seeing where I was or what was around me. I now found I was not only seeing where I was and my surroundings, but they looked clearer, brighter, more wonderful than I could have once imagined.

Much has been said about being in the present, in the now, and experiencing life from that perspective. We can't actually be anywhere but in the now, but we can become aware of that fact. When we live each instant with awareness of the moment, not allowing our minds to focus on the past or future, we allow ourselves to fully enjoy every experience.

I arrived at the Grand Canyon in late morning, with streaked white clouds drifting through light blue sky. I had been there as a child and again six years earlier, and the changes in the area were enormous. Outside the entrance, where there was once only trees and nature, there is now lodging, restaurants, and even an IMAX Theatre.

Lodging and shops are built right on the rim, and done in such a wonderful synchronization of nature that they do not take away from the beauty, but yet enhance it. I was impressed. Often when modernization takes place it is at the expense of the natural wonders, but was not so in this case.

As a child I had watched the mules in the park descend the canyon walls on narrow paths built for the not so feint of heart. Now I stood on these same paths, hiking down the side of the canyon. Standing on the edge of the path and seeing the drop-off to my side was a unique experience. One step to the side would have been a very large step indeed, descending to the canyon bottom, so many thousand feet below. I realized how tenuous our stay in this world really is. Staying on this path would keep me grounded in this third dimensional reality, while stepping to the side would have brought me to another reality completely. I chose to stay close to the wall!

Walking and driving the South Rim is something not to be missed. Vistas of natural brilliance stretch as far as the eye can see. A palette of browns, reds, blues, and greens cannot match this to perfection. Sky meets the opposite rim in a homogenized wash of color, blue on blue. Striated formations of reds, browns, and blues fill the massive canyon below, forming every shape and form you could imagine. Hills, peaks, and crevasses abound, with stunted, bent, and twisted trees lining the rim.

Miles and miles of similar views filled the visual field. A river, the Colorado, meanders through this magical wonderland, an aqua line of liquid paint on a canvas of diverse tones beneath the clouded sky, muted in humble reverence and surrender to the world above. Words were not needed, for the heart spoke its own, in witness with God.

I found that I observed more when I was by myself, but the experience was less pleasurable without someone to share it. It is one of the things I had not previously considered. There is a joy beyond words when we connect with God, and yet there is loneliness when we have no other human to share experience with. It is a paradox I am still in wonderment about. Joy is from within; pleasure is shared in the physical world. We need both to maintain balance in our lives.

I left the canyon in the afternoon and headed into the desert. Travelling through open, rolling desert was another change from the mountains and forests. Without the interruption of trees and mountains, the horizon stretched for what seemed like forever. I began to laugh as I watched the sky, wondering if there were other civilizations out there and decided that if there were, and if they did come to visit, this would be the world's largest UFO parking lot.

I reached Winslow about five fifteen with fatigue beginning

to set in. I was exhausted. I wanted to have a leisurely meal so I asked the hotel attendant where there was a good place to have some authentic Mexican food. He sent me to a small, local restaurant, just a few tables in a large open room. The atmosphere was not impressive, but the food was the best I had ever experienced. It was a perfect ending for yet another perfect day.

Conversation with The Guys:

Pat: I used the technique I learned in Sedona today and the connection with you felt much better. It feels solid and pure. Is there anything you would like to tell me?

Guys: Your life purpose is to heal the energy imbalance of yourself and then the world at large. This will be done with the allegiance, acceptance and free will of those that sub-scribe to this wisdom. As with all things, it must not be forced upon another. It must be brought to the attention, with intention, and left to them to take or leave.

We know you have many questions about what you will be doing with this. As with all things, free will is no less true for you. You have enormous potential, but you must now turn the focus away from yourself and turn it to the world.

You will be given the opportunity to help many. Whether you choose to do this is your choice alone. You need only come to this place and ask and you shall receive. It is that simple.

Keep it as pure as you can. You will learn, with practice, when you are with us and when you are not. You will know by how it feels. Learn to feel us. There will be no error here. Answers will be given as you ask. You are the person in charge. We cannot do anything unless you ask. We feel you beginning to understand the profound depth of this. When you understand this, clarity opens up.

Pat: Is there more to do here or is it time to go home?

Guys: It is up to you. There is much being accomplished. Do what feels right for you. We urge you to do as much inner work as possible while you can. Go with peace in your heart Dear One and know that love is all there is. The more you spend time in this state, the more you will help others to do the same. Love yourself and others will feel it and learn to love themselves.

Lesson from the day: Gratefulness

We spend most of each day going about our usual routines and paying no attention to what is in front of us. We do not take the time to notice what is there and even less being grateful for any of it. We do this while driving, at work, doing daily chores and any other thing we can think of.

It is time to change the way we look at life. Without seeing what is there and seeing the value in it, life is a boring, repetitive sequence of motions. We become little robots going about our days without any connection to the life we are living. It is time to remove the blinders we have covering our eyes and the shields we have hiding our hearts.

When you experience the connection with the life around you, you see how important these things are to your life in ways you never though possible. Be grateful for all of these things, for without them, you have nothing. Without this outer world, your experience of life becomes sterile, cold and lonely.

When you forget this, remember these few tips.

1. Notice what is around you. See the scenery. Feel the water and the grass. Hear the birds.

2. Feel the energy of everything around you.

3. Do not let fear of being hurt stop you from loving what is there AND being loved by it!

4. Realize you are not alone. You are part of this great soup of energy, mixing, mingling and learning from each other.

5. Be grateful for the company. It is the most valuable commodity in the universe.

Day Fifteen
Recycled Energy

I awoke in the morning with a feeling of restlessness. Even though I was experiencing an adventure beyond my wildest imagination, I was getting tired. There were two places on my mind that I felt a need to see. One was Petrified Forest and the other was Canyon de Chelly (pronounced de shay). I had to drive past the first to go north to the second, so I figured I'd stop and run through Petrified Forest as quickly as I could. I was in for yet one more surprise.

I stopped at the first entrance I came to. It was an eighteen-mile drive from the highway and I was becoming impatient. I tried to center myself and connect with the inner peace within and got the question – "What's your hurry"? I had no answer. As I entered the park, I stopped a the Visitor Center. Behind the building was a path leading into a section of the desert that was littered with fallen, petrified trees.

A large expanse of desert stretched before me, rolling hills and flat desert littered with fallen trees of rock, glistening in the sun. Tree trunks in shades of blues, browns, yellows, greens and reds, sparkled in the light like embedded jewels held there for eons, now peeking from their hiding place.

About two hundred and twenty five million years ago the area was a vast floodplain. Huge pine and other stately trees surrounded the water. Dinosaurs, crocodile-like reptiles, giant fish eating amphibians and other such beings roamed the area. Large ferns and other water loving plants grew unrestrained.

Eventually silt, mud and volcanic ash covered the area, burying the logs and cutting off the oxygen supply. They started to decay and silica-bearing groundwater seeped through, replacing the wood with silica deposits. This crystallized into quartz and the logs were preserved as petrified wood.

Petrified tree

Today erosion continues to unearth these magnificent wonders of creation, bringing us a picture of a world that once was. I was drawn to walk this path and I came to the edge of a cliff overlooking an area so vast, it challenged the imagination. I could almost smell the dank trees and sulfa and see the dinosaurs roaming, roaring their presence to the world around them.

There were few people in the park that morning, affording me a quiet, peaceful union with my surroundings. Sitting on the edge of the cliff, looking out to the horizon, I felt the connection to the world around me. I decided to try the technique I had learned in Sedona and connect to God, All That Is. The message I received was this: "You stand in the energy of your predecessors. They are here still, yet their form has changed. They will be with you always. Remember that ONLY the form has changed, the energy remains. This was a hub of activity for my creatures – AND STILL IS! You must know that only the form changes. The energy now is the same energy as then, RECYCLED. It has changed many times and will yet more. ALL is ONE."

As I sat there on that rock ledge, looking out at eons of changing structure, I felt something in me shift. The impatience and some old tension and worry were being dissolved in a pool of serenity. The world was different, and yet I knew it was the same. I remembered a lesson I had once received about the water we drink today being the same water the dinosaurs drank and I knew this to be true. It changes form, from ice, to water, to steam, and returns once more.

Energy can neither be created nor destroyed. It is eternal and forevermore. Energy becomes visible when the vibration slows to a certain level. As with water, when we raise the vibration it becomes steam and disappears from view. When we take the same water and slow down the vibration, it becomes mass, or ice. It is the same for humans. We are, according to Einstein, frozen energy. So it is with all things physical. Ashes to ashes; dust to dust. We cannot die, we can only change form.

My head was swirling with this principle of energy physics and spirituality. I began to see all the things that seemed so impermanent to me in the past, and saw them from a different perspective. The dinosaurs live on in us as we will live on in our successors. I understood the four Laws of Creation, which I believe to be true.

1. We exist. We are energy, spirit. We are Divine Essence, unchangeable, eternal, and forevermore.

2. The One is All, and the All is One. We are but a piece of the ALL, and we are all of the piece. We are holographic. We are a cell in the body of God, a quantum particle of that All Knowing Consciousness. We are pieces of God, experiencing Itself.

3. What we give out, we get back. This has been called many things, such as Karma. Do unto others as you would have them done unto you.

4. Change is the only constant. Everything changes, except the first three laws.

These are things I believe to be constant in any place in the Universe, the Multiverse. I believe that God created everything in the multiverse, not just us. We are all the same, all together, all one. Other laws that we create are for the benefit of the people they are created for, and will be different for different people and situations. What is beneficial for one society may not be for another. The same is true for time. The laws that worked for one time period may no longer work in another.

Most of that day was spent hiking the desert in this awesome place. Time and impatience was forgotten as wonderment replaced a sense of complacency. I was once again seeing what it means to "become as little children". Children look at everything as a new thing. They are in a constant state of wonder. I believe we need to become more like that, to forget the meanings we have put on everything and see it as a child would see it.

The eastern end of the Petrified Forest is called the Painted Desert and looks like pointed hills that someone spilled buckets of earthy colored paint on, brushing it horizontally across the landscape. I stopped at one overlook with a path down to the valley floor. It was hot and I hiked only a partial distance to the bottom and for some reason felt a need to turn around. Back at the top, I met a woman who was pregnant with twins. Her husband and other children had gone down the path and were not due back for about half an hour.

We talked as if we had known one another for eons and I found myself asking if she knew what "Indigo Children" are. She said no and was immensely interested. I explained how they are advanced souls and challenging our populace to find new teaching methods. Many have been diagnosed as having Attention Deficit Disorder. I told her of the book called "The Indigo Children", by Lee Carol and Jan Tober and she said she was going to find the book. As soon as we discussed this, her family returned. They were twenty minutes early. We knew we had shared what we needed to share and said our good byes.

This was one more thing I knew was not coincidence. For some reason we were placed there together at exactly the right time for that conversation. I have often wondered about her twins and how she is doing. I would not be at all surprised to know that her twins fit into the category of these children. I once more thanked God for the opportunity to be student and teacher. As I received, I gave, always the dance of energy from one place to another, in perfect balance.

Driving north through the desert toward Canyon de Chelly, I came to Hubbell Trading Post, now a National Park site. It is the oldest continuously operating trading post in the Navajo Nation. It was started and run by a man named John Lorenzo Hubbell and flourished in the late eighteen and early nineteen hundreds. He was known for his fair dealings with the Navajo people and even helped with the smallpox epidemic, using his house as a hospital. I did not have time to see it all but if you like stepping back into White/Native American history, this is a great place to visit.

It was getting late, and I chose to push on to Canyon de Chelly, arriving there in the evening. I was exhausted and chose to relax in a comforting bubble bath, allowing the effervescent bubbles to dissolve the tension of the moment. Fatigue took front row in my awareness and I went to sleep that night feeling at peace with myself.

Conversation with The Guys:

Pat: What is happening to me today? I feel so different.

Guys: You are finding home within yourself. Fear not the encumbrances of your own definitions and boundaries that you set for yourself. There is more to all of you than meets the eye. You all went there to experience what it is like to live in free will so you can work through the issues you have accrued from past experience.

Know it is commendable that you chose such a challenging course. We know it is difficult to maintain your composure and equilibrium from that confined view of reality.

Today you saw beyond the 3-D view and broadened it to hold the greater vision. You stopped judgment of your actions and took the time to just BE.

Pat: How can I help others to do the same?

Guys: Only they can choose to do so. You can bring them the stories of your own experiences and they will choose whether or not to enlighten their own selves. You are pioneering many things for the masses. You can NOT make them do as you do. You CAN show them the way and let them choose for themselves.

Pat: Thank you.

Guys: Thank yourself Dear One, for it is your own choice

that has put you where you are this day.

Pat: Who, or what, are the energies that I have been spending time with, the ones who distorted the truth?

Guys: They are "hitchhikers." These are beings that see light and hitch a ride, so to speak. They like to get their energy from those who are bright. If you find yourself feeling uncomfortable with a message and question where it is from, raise your energy to what you remember we feel like. This will call us. We will tell you the truth. You are in control and have the power to recognize us. You need never give your power to another again.

Lesson from the day:
Life is a circle, returning again and again.

When we view ourselves as the body we inhabit, life becomes finite. We believe that when it does what we call "dying," we are no longer still here. This is as far from the truth as possible. The body is a manifestation of who we are in reality, not the other way around.

We are taught that we have one life and believe it ends when we leave our body. We do have one life and that life is eternal. Religion teaches many versions of this truth. Some believe we continue our one true life in other life experiences. This can be known as reincarnation or parallel lives. Some believe we are born at birth of this body and leave for Heaven or Hell when we die. There are many more beliefs.

It does not matter what we believe. We are eternal and that cannot change. How we choose to believe it manifests is up to us. We may not know for sure until we return to our true home of spirit and soul, but we can know we do not end here. Just as the water changes form and returns, so shall we.

1. Give yourself permission to question what you have been taught.

2. Be open to other's who believe differently than you. Could it be they may be correct?

3. Feel these things in your heart and soul and adopt the beliefs that work for you.

4. Be open to past life, alternate life, and other beliefs you may not believe as yet.

5. See birth as a choice to experience separation in a physical body.

6. See death as a doorway, not an end.

7. Entertain the thought that you will live to experience MANY more things, in ways you cannot yet imagine.

Day Sixteen
A Step into the Past

I awoke with a feeling of completion. This adventure was turning out to be more than I had expected and I knew it was coming to an end. I would soon be heading home. I spent part of the morning viewing Canyon de Chelly from the thirty six mile south rim. If I had an expectation of what this would look like, it did not fit, could not fit. I had never seen anything like it. It was awesome, and it was very different from anything else I had seen.

Canyon de Chelly

The Grand Canyon had been huge and expansive in its scope. This was narrow and deep, but no less spectacular. Tall, steep cliffs line the walls, the canyon twisting and turning its way between them. At the bottom, a dusty brown dirt road traverses the canyon floor, surrounded by lush gardens and greenery. I was once again being challenged to overcome my definitions. This was a canyon of a different kind and of rare magnificence.

There is a cliff dwelling that can be viewed near the bottom of the steep wall. This can be seen from below or from the rim as I viewed it. There is a path that leads down into the canyon and it is possible to walk to the site. I had a driving need to leave and head back for New Mexico that day, so I chose to view it from above. It was no less spectacular.

Tall spires of rock, reaching the height of the rim, stood sentry over the canyon in reverential silence. There was an energy, a feeling from this place of timelessness. It felt untouched in the overall scheme of things, untouched and unchanged, although I knew that was not so. It felt old, like the elders with all their accumulated wisdom lived on in those walls. They emanated love and life and eternity.

Heading north, the desert once more changed. Flat, reddish-brown terrain became dotted with tall spires of earth, reaching toward the sky. Some were flattened over time, mesas, overlooking the floor below. Others reached heaven-ward with sharpened points and uneven edges. Had I been in a cave, it would have reminded me of stalagmites, growing up from their earthen core, reaching for the heavens.

The "Four Corners" is unique in that it is a place in our country where four states come together. Arizona, Utah, New Mexico, and Colorado converge in one neat union. A short distance from there is "Ship Rock", a formation rising seventeen hundred feet from the desert floor and it is sacred to the Navajo. It is also easy to imagine the settlers in their covered wagons celebrating as they approached this landmark on their journey west.

The need to go home was becoming stronger as the day went on. My mother was having a family reunion in three days and I had thought I would have to miss it. I no longer found that an acceptable option. I would continue to see all I could that day and then try to change my return flight to be there for my mother. I knew it would be a grueling schedule for the next two days, but believed I could manage it.

Once more in New Mexico, I chose to visit Chaco Canyon that afternoon and headed south. I arrived at the entrance about three thirty and drove the sixteen miles of dirt road to the visitor center. I crossed a ravine that was lined with a cement slab and accompanied by a sign that said if water was running on this slab, not to drive over it. I took the warning seriously, as arroyos in this area are known to flood very rapidly.

Chaco Culture National Historic Park is awesome. One of the pueblos, Pueblo Bonito is situated at the base of a cliff. It is the most spectacular ruin I have ever seen. It is in high desert country, with long winters, short growing seasons, and very little rainfall. A thousand years ago it was a center of community life. The monumental masonry buildings were built in a horseshoe shape, with the curve facing a cliff, placed within a landscape surrounded by sacred mountains, mesas, and shrines that still have deep spiritual meaning for American Indian descendants.

It eventually towered four stories high and contained over six hundred rooms and forty kivas, or sacred ceremonial rooms, made in circular fashion. The living quarters were interconnected, a forerunner of today's apartment buildings, one leading to the next. Doorways were of many heights and some I had to bend over to get through. Walking through the rooms brought a feeling I cannot convey in mere words. I could almost hear chanting and drums, the sounds of women cooking, children playing, dogs yipping, and men conducting ceremonies in the kivas.

Pueblo Bonito ruin

Many of the structures were designed orienting to lunar, solar, and cardinal directions. Sophisticated astronomical markers surrounded the community. Here I was, once again, standing in an astronomically designed environment. For some reason I was being led to a large number of places that connected earth and sky. First I was to see this in the modern world of telescopes and then in the older version of an ancient wisdom we can only hypothesize.

I was told by my teacher in Sedona that if I visited Chaco Canyon, I needed to do a channeling and connect with God, the Universe, while I was there. I did so and got this message: "This is sacred space. Walk not on feet of clay, but yet on feet of light." I kept hearing the same words as I walked through the ruins. "Walk on feet of light." I understood that I needed to see myself, and all beings, as light, pure energy, and as spirit, not just as the physical beings we see with our physical eyes.

I would like to have spent much more time exploring the ruins and adjacent area with its myriad of interconnecting roads, linking other communities to this major one. As I watched the sky however, I knew this would not be possible. A large storm was approaching rapidly and the sky was becoming filled with black clouds, lightning shooting from their depths. Remembering the arroyo I had crossed, I headed quickly for the entrance.

The drive back became a race for time, as the storm loomed ever closer. I crossed the cement slab just as water began to move on its surface and as I climbed the hill away from this depression, the sky seemed to open upon me. Great torrents of rain fell from these clouds and thunder rolled as lightning lit the skies. I had to stop for a while, as I was unable to see through the heavy rain, the windshield wipers unable to keep up with the deluge.

I drove onward toward Bernalillo, thoughts racing in my mind. I had been given so many gifts on this journey and did not want it to end. At the same time, I could not wait to go home. I also wondered where my home was. I knew I would be going back, but it did not feel like I would be going *home*. Something had significantly changed. Me. **I** would not be going home. The person returning to my house and family was no longer the same person who left it just over two weeks earlier. A lifetime had elapsed in that short time.

I stopped in a small town for something to eat and got what had become my favorite treat on this adventure – a Corn Dog and Root Beer Float. Not exactly the greatest nutritional meal, but it could have passed for the world's finest wine and filet mignon at that moment. I was complete.

I arrived in Bernalillo late that evening and called the airline. It would cost one hundred dollars to change my return flight date and I decided it would be worth it to be home for my mother's party. I called her to tell her the news and she was ecstatic. I also called home and talked with my husband. We had concerns about schedule differences upon my return, as I was returning early, and I realized I had little patience.

My pattern had always been to make everything work, to try to fix everything and make things all better. Over the years I had lost myself in the pattern of taking care of everyone and everything else. I was learning that this is impossible. We can make choices for ourselves, but we cannot make anyone or anything else "all better - or worse," without their permission. I needed to be true to myself, even if it meant others not being happy with my choices. I knew my return would bring more changes than I could imagine. I fell into bed with mixed feelings vying for position in my awareness and fell into a deep, exhausted sleep.

Conversation with The Guys:

Pat: I am concerned about going home. I do not know what to do with my marriage and with my life.

Guys: Take it one moment at a time. One thing will lead to the next as it needs to be. Do not get caught up in worry over something that has not yet been created.

Pat: I now see that this is not about me. It is about the bigger picture of humanity and how we are evolving.

Guys: It is about you as far as what role you play. The play itself is much larger and is NOT about you. It will happen with or without you. Always keep your focus and remember to keep things in perspective.

You were not working up to your potential. Now you are. The connection you now feel with us will be growing in ways you have yet to imagine.

Lesson from the day: Walk on feet of LIGHT

We walk on feet every day. What does it mean to walk on feet of light? It means we have to remember that we are made up of more than just photons and force fields. We have to remember that we are Spirit and Soul. When we remember this AND walk and talk this truth, we become more than we ever thought we could be.

This is when we move from living our lives like automatons, robots, to living fully and consciously. From there we are able to use our free will to create the highest version of ourselves we can be. When we do that, everyone around us gets the advantage of learning how to do that also. We are the examples for everyone else to see, as they are for us.

It is easy to get caught up in playing the role of being lost in the dark. We stumble around and stub our toes as we seek the light. We already ARE the light. We cannot be anything BUT that. We can, however, forget that and walk on feet of clay. We need to open our eyes and our minds and see what our Soul sees so we can walk on feet of LIGHT.

To do this, remember these few thoughts:

1. Know that you already ARE the light you seek.

2. Remember that in the dark moments as well as the happy ones.

3. Look at yourself and see if you are living what you believe.

4. If you are not, what can you change to be true to yourself?

5. Walk and talk your truth.

Day Seventeen
Coming Full Circle

I slept a little later in the morning and tried to take in all the things that had been happening so far. It was impossible to do, so I decided to just let it filter down as it needed to. I would know when the time came to understand.

I had heard of a place north of Santa Fe, called El Santuario de Chimayo. It is a small mission, built in the mountains and called the "Lourdes of America." Legend has it that around the year eighteen twelve, a member of the local church was walking in the hills and saw a light springing from the ground. He dug with his bare hands and found the shining light to be a crucifix.

He notified the priest and a procession retrieved the crucifix, bringing it back to the church. The next morning it was gone and was once again found in its original position in the ground in the hills. This repeated itself three times and they decided it was a sign to build a chapel on the original location in the hills.

It is a beautiful little chapel, filled with ornately decorated wooden religious relics. One room has notes from people who say they have been cured of all types of ailments. There is an outside chapel area with benches and a small village and gift shop. People now come from all over the world to see this chapel and take a handful of dirt, which is purported to have healing qualities.

Traveling in the mountainous area was a challenge with or without the map and I found myself wandering for a part of the morning, looking for the chapel. Even so, it was a restful change from the traveling of the last several days. I had time to take a breath and unwind, reminding me again that we need to rest and recharge our batteries often, or we will create illness that will **make** us stop and get the rest we need.

El Santuario de Chimayo

There were shops scattered throughout the mountains selling pottery and hand-made woven products. There was a beautiful black on black pottery healing bowl, made by a Pueblo that is famous for the technique. I bought it and filled it with dirt from the chapel at Chimayo. It sits in daily view to remind me of our miraculous healing potential.

The last place I visited was Santa Fe. I needed to do some last minute shopping and wanted to end this adventure in one of my favorite places. I walked the plaza and thought about the things that had happened since I left there two weeks earlier. It felt like a lifetime, and yet it seemed like it happened in a blink. This journey was coming to an end and I felt like I would be leaving an old friend. I also knew it would be months before I would be able to assimilate all I had experienced.

This time the energy of the town felt much calmer and I enjoyed my time there immensely. I was no longer in a hurry to get where I was going, but returning from a journey that filled my heart with joy.

I returned to the same motel in Albuquerque that I had stayed in on the first day. It seemed fitting somehow, to return to the point at which I began. I had come full circle. I was happy to be going home, and I was sad to be leaving such a wonderful part of my life. I had learned here, grown here, and had fallen in love with this land.

I spent the evening packing my belongings. As always, I had more to go home with than I had arrived with. When that was accomplished and manageable, I crawled into bed and spent my last night in a land that had stolen my heart. I will always have a special love for the Southwest. It had become a part of my very being.

Conversation with The Guys:

Pat: Well, this is it. Tomorrow I go home. Is there anything I need to know before I go?

Guys: Take a piece of this love with you, for it is you. You have spent time here and given of yourself as well as received. All is in balance.

Take home the wisdom you have gained from this experience and do with it what will make you the happiest. We would like you to know that you will not be the same as you were before. The changes may seem subtle, but they are larger than you think. Allow for these changes to find a comfortable place. Know that you are better for the experience, and many others are better for it also. You have touched many, as you have been touched.

Do not be shy. It is time to go forward and create a path for yourself that is conducive to your joy. You have been sitting at home waiting for things to land in your lap. You have to also make inroads and efforts to that goal.

Be bold. Step out and be seen. It is now time for movement and action. You have the answers. You have the resources. You just have to find them and put them into action.

Do as you did here. Let one thing lead to the next, for it shall surely happen in that manner. Allow it. Step aside and let it happen. Ask and you shall receive.

Now we ask that you get some rest and relax. Be kind to yourself and know that soon you will reach a level of which you had not yet dreamed – IF you allow yourself to. Always, always, always go to your highest source. We know you have that one learned well, but you have yet to feel it as a part of yourself.

Lesson from the day:
Create a sense of completion

This may seem like a strange lesson, but it is so very important. So often in life, we have experiences that leave us feeling like something is missing. It is important, paramount, that we bring them to completion so we can go on unencumbered.

I have had relationships that I worked very hard to resolve and bring to completion so I could move forward with a sense of peace. When I did not do that, there was always a feeling of unrest and a wish that I could have done more. When I worked through the things that kept me from resolution and let them go, I was able to close the circle and feel love in my soul.

We need to find the loose ends and tie them up whenever we can. It is important to not leave a situation, be it a journey or a relationship, without knowing you have done all you can and that you are happy with yourself.

If you find yourself uncomfortable leaving a person, place or thing, follow these steps:

1. Notice what you are uncomfortable about.

2. Come up with workable solutions as to how to resolve the situation.

3. If it is not possible to resolve it with the other person, come to peace with it in you. WITHOUT GUILT.

4. Know that you can bring all the happy things of the situation with you.

5. Know you can leave the painful ones behind.

6. Know that you completed your task with your head held high and love in your heart. Someone else may not see it the same way. Let that be OK. You can only choose joy for you. Everyone else chooses their own – or they do not.

Day Eighteen
Home

Sadness filled my heart as the runway fell away from view. Outside the plane window, the now familiar mountains and desert sped by as we climbed higher and higher, the details blurring into a homogenous mix of color. I began to feel numb from all the mixed emotions that were swirling around in my being. Joy, sadness, fear and wonder mixed into one unrecognized emotion. The familiar life I had left behind was about to become the unfamiliar, as I returned. Nothing could ever be the same because I was no longer who I had been.

Epilogue

I had been hoping that I would go home, get off the airplane, meet my husband, and everything would be all better. As we all know, things do not always work that way. The better had turned to worse. We were no longer able to hide the depth of our differences and chose to go our separate ways.

Home, as I experienced on that gypsum dune in New Mexico, is a relative term. Returning to my house and family turned out to be a continuation of the previous eighteen days. My house was a place, but not the home it once was. Many things were happening within my family structure and I never made it out of my suitcase. It was as if the Universe had other plans for me and I bounced from place to place.

Life is always, all ways a challenge. I used to think that challenge had to be hard, but now know that it can be smooth when we allow it to be. We need to let life flow through us like a river. There are times the river runs over rocks and around sharp bends on the riverbanks, but as long as we build no dams, the flow is smooth. It is when we create resistance to the flow that we create pain for ourselves.

We are the creators of our own lives. We create in each and every moment, with each and every choice. When I was a child it seemed like this was not true because it took a long time to see the results of my actions. Today the world is changing and we see the results much sooner, if not immediately. This shows up in our world in many ways. We now watch war on television, live and in color. The internet gives us immediate answers to our questions. Drive-up windows give us immediate results for food, money, and pharmaceuticals.

I once thought there were two answers for everything,

right and wrong, good and bad, and all other opposites. We live in a world of duality and see polarity the most clearly. I am finding there is not only black and white, but a whole range of grays and magnificent colors in between. Things are not this OR that, but this AND that.

Each thing we see out there is true and real for someone. Your truth may not be my truth, but it is as true for you as mine is for me. We make rules, laws and regulations to keep order in a society, but personal beliefs are something we cannot regulate. Religion is a perfect example. There are many in our world and I see none of them as THE right one. I feel that all who believe in God, a higher power, and who worship with love and peaceful intention are the same, but seen from a different perspective, a different point of view.

The same is true for all things in our world. I saw many things and met many people on my adventure. They were from many different backgrounds, races, colors, creeds, and beliefs. There remains one thing that brings us all together. We are all made up of the same thing. We are all souls here for the same purpose – to remember who we are, to grow and learn, to love ourselves and each other.

I was given the gift of understanding this principle on my eighteen-day adventure. Being by myself was a gift beyond my wildest dreams. I was not alone, for that is impossible. We are never alone. We need to take the time to be private and feel the love of the Universe, of God, within our hearts. If we all did that, war and conflict would disappear. Disease would become a thing of the past. Joy would replace sorrow and pain.

When I watch the news now and see that war and conflict are still a part of our world, I see there is still a part of me that needs to change. Ninety-nine percent of me is appalled, and yet there is that one percent that roots for one side or the other. As long as that is there, I am as responsible as the one pulling the trigger. Hatred does not start out there, but in us. When that is gone, war will be a thing of the past.

Peace begins within us. When we are happy with ourselves it will radiate to those around us and it will spread. As I sat in company of the Universe and felt the connection to All That Is, I felt the presence of something greater than what I see in the physical mirror. It is the mirror we see around us in every-day life that shows us who we are. We need to take the time, make the time to see what is there and take responsibility for our part in creating it.

How do we do this? Do we all need to take a trip into the desert as I did? No. The trip into the desert was a living example of what is possible for all of us. We can start by setting aside ten minutes a day and sitting in silence or with soft music for background. Walk in the woods, on a beach, or down a country lane. Be aware of your surroundings. In your mind, talk with the trees and animals, and if you sense they answer you – smile.

Laugh, play and watch the little children. If we have not yet taught them otherwise, they will teach us how to love. They also teach us who and what we are. As they play, we see them act out what they see in their homes and the world around them. We need to take responsibility for what they learn from us. As we change, so will they.

Dependence is another thing I found to be different upon my return. I had become very independent, and yet I found that dependence and independence are two sides of the same one thing. One is being dependent on another for your needs; the other is being dependent on yourself. Knowing I could do this trip by myself taught me I am responsible to myself in all aspects of life. I am no longer willing to give away responsibility for myself to someone else or to take on responsibility for someone else.

We are all responsible to ourselves. Responsibility is the ability to respond. We are not responsible *for* things, but *to* them. When we confuse the two and try to be responsible for others, we take away their power to be responsible to themselves. I had confused the two for years and thought I had to take care of everyone. I now allow others to have their own power and responsibility.

This does not mean letting them go or not caring. It means caring enough to let them grow. It is much like watching a child learn to walk. When they fall it is sometimes necessary to let them get back up by themselves so they know they can do it. If they are hurt we can guide them to get the help they need. We can give love and be there to help them grow in their own confidence. It is paramount that we do not take away their power.

We hold the potential of Heaven on Earth within us. We can choose joy or sadness in each moment. A great friend and teacher once said, "Choose joy, for no reason." It is always when we feel the worst, when we are in the middle of personal crises that we forget to see the sun. That is when we most need to look beyond the dark cloud and choose to see the light. Never doubt in darkness what you believe in light.

These were only a few of the changes that took place within me when I returned. My life is forever changed. There are still days of fear and loneliness as I work through issues that are kicked up from time to time, but I would not change a thing. I am learning and growing with each new day.

I asked for a prayer that would help me with these changes in my daily life and was given this:

"God, help me to free myself from all the self-imposed restrictions and judgments I have made. Help me to hold myself in the palm of my hand and see the beauty of my self, to love that self and honor the presence and divinity of this love. Help me to know the value of my self, to honor and cherish it in each moment. Let me know who I am, to BE who I am in each moment, to live this with all my heart and soul.

Let me remember these things when the path becomes difficult, when my doubts and human frailties obscure the light. Help me to see the light in the darkness, the glimmer of hope in the most frightening of times. Let me always see you, feel you in every moment. Let me know that I am you, a holographic representation of the whole in this piece called me.

I am yours in heart, in spirit, in body and mind. I am yours to mold as your own, your messenger in space and time. Help me, in all ways, to keep this awareness and use this for the mutual benefit of all. For this I pray oh Lord, for all these things I pray. AMEN."

Made in the USA
Lexington, KY
23 March 2012